Native American Boarding Schools

Native American Boarding Schools

Mary A. Stout

Landmarks of the American Mosaic

GREENWOOD

AN IMPRINT OF ABC-CLIO, LLC
Santa Barbara, California • Denver, Colorado • Oxford, England

Library of Congress Cataloging-in-Publication Data

Stout, Mary, 1954–
    Native American boarding schools / Mary A. Stout.
        p. cm. — (Landmarks of the American mosaic)
    Includes bibliographical references and index.
    ISBN 978-0-313-38676-3 (hardcopy : alk. paper) — ISBN 978-0-313-38677-0 (ebook)   1. Off-reservation boarding schools—United States—History—Juvenile literature.   2. Indian children—Relocation—United States—History—Juvenile literature.   3. Indian children—Education—Juvenile literature.   4. Indians, Treatment of—United States—History—Juvenile literature.   I. Title.
    E97.5.S76   2012
    371.829'97073—dc23   2011051895

ISBN: 978-0-313-38676-3
EISBN: 978-0-313-38677-0

16   15   14   13   12   1   2   3   4   5

This book is also available on the World Wide Web as an eBook.
Visit www.abc-clio.com for details.

Greenwood
An Imprint of ABC-CLIO, LLC

ABC-CLIO, LLC
130 Cremona Drive, P.O. Box 1911
Santa Barbara, California 93116-1911

This book is printed on acid-free paper ∞

Manufactured in the United States of America

Contents

Series Foreword

THE LANDMARKS OF THE AMERICAN MOSAIC series comprises individual volumes devoted to exploring an event or development central to this country's multicultural heritage. The topics illuminate the struggles and triumphs of American Indians, African Americans, Latinos, and Asian Americans, from European contact through the turbulent last half of the 20th century. The series covers landmark court cases, laws, government programs, civil rights infringements, riots, battles, movements, and more. Written by historians especially for high-school students on up and general readers, these content-rich references satisfy more thorough research needs and provide a deeper understanding of material that students might only otherwise be exposed to in a short section in a textbook or superficial explanation online.

Each book on a particular topic is a one-stop reference source. The series format includes

- Introduction
- Chronology
- Narrative chapters that trace the evolution of the event or topic chronologically
- Biographical profiles of key figures
- Selection of crucial primary documents
- Glossary
- Annotated Bibliography
- Index

This landmark series promotes respect for cultural diversity and supports the social studies curriculum by helping students understand multicultural American history.

Preface

THE NOTION THAT THE UNITED STATES OF AMERICA sought to forcefully assimilate the native inhabitants that they had recently conquered by force and consigned to unwanted bits of real estate, by gathering a generation or so of their young children into large, unfriendly institutional boarding schools, is quite horrifying to think about these days. It is often a subject quickly passed over in U.S. history, I assume, due to the shame and embarrassment that exists because the government promulgated this policy. It was ethnocide, or cultural genocide, and that was the boarding school experience at its best.

One of the key things learned by studying this important aspect of U.S. history, is that this effort to eradicate Native American culture and language was not particularly successful. The Native American children and families involved in the boarding school movement were not passive vessels to be filled or broken during the boarding school assimilation and acculturation process. They were not dolls, and they did not necessarily fulfill the program of turning them into white Americans. Rather, each person who attended boarding school had a different reaction and a different opinion about the process. Many of them figured out who they were at boarding school, and who they were was "Indian."

While it is hard to imagine, some of the boarding schools actually survived to become residential high schools or even colleges today. Somewhere along the line, they were embraced by the very people that they were created to destroy, and turned into something that works for them, something that symbolizes Native America, by some sort of amazing human alchemy. The stories of the students attending boarding schools are all different and complex, with hidden depths. The boarding school experience was not uniform; it was multidimensional. And the students who lived through boarding schools tell astonishing stories of courage, resistance, and adaptation.

This book is a reference work for contemporary students interested in the topic of Native American boarding schools in the United States. The early chapters address the mission schools of the early settlers among the American Indians, the precursors of the government boarding schools. Chapter Three focuses on young Colonel Richard Pratt's grand experiment at Carlisle Indian School, the first of the off-reservation government boarding schools. Pratt's school became the model for all of the succeeding government boarding schools.

The boarding schools changed through the decades with legal and social changes, and several chapters show the change over time by highlighting the story of one student at one school during that period of time. In the end, the boarding schools closed down or were transformed, as the U.S. government slowly recognized that they were not only ineffective, but damaging to the students. The manner of educating Native American students is finally coming full circle as tribal control of schools becomes the order of the day. After contemporary Native American education is addressed, the final chapter looks at some of the outcomes of the boarding school education.

Finally, there are special materials such as a chronology, a glossary of terms, biographies of key people, and an annotated bibliography of sources for this topic.

Acknowledgments

Many people have helped me with the research for this book, but I would especially like to thank Dr. K. Tsianina Lomawaima, an educator and scholar in the field, who was most generous with her time and with her suggestions. Of course, any mistakes are all mine, but her wisdom and insight were valued and appreciated.

This book is dedicated to my mother and father, Marge and Jim Stout. Our parents are our first and primary teachers, no matter what culture you are born into.

Introduction

THROUGH COUNTLESS STORIES, letters, and oral histories, along with dry institutional records and government reports, the history of Native American children's education in boarding schools is revealed. Although the individual experiences were as different and as numerous as the children experiencing them, the significance of their experiences, and how they would shape history, can only be appreciated when there is some knowledge of the traditional Native American educational system.

Prior to European contact, traditional Native American education varied from tribe to tribe and place to place. Although documentation is not complete, we believe that the focus of traditional Native American education, which was taken very seriously by the people, was first and foremost survival in the environment in which the tribe lived. Also, the transmission of a very rich culture in a nonliterate society demanded a strong and dedicated oral history program. Those European Americans who assumed that no educational practices existed within traditional tribes, and sought to replace nothing with something, were wrong in their assumptions. It is difficult to generalize about Native American educational practices, because North America was populated with more than 500 different cultures speaking more than 300 different languages. Autobiographies of Native Americans who experienced a traditional upbringing and education within their tribes provide a window onto some of the basic educational practices.

Luther Standing Bear wrote of his early education in *My Indian Boyhood*, published in 1931. He describes how young boys made small bows and arrows and played hunting games in his Lakota community. It was not unusual for young children's play to mimic the more serious tasks of the adults, and children learned how to hide in the forest, approach game slowly, and accurately throw stones long before they became adept bow-and-arrow hunters. Standing Bear outlines how he mastered horsemanship, hunting, fishing, and the tanning of hides. He also learned in depth about the natural world around him and the history and governance of his tribe. Standing Bear concluded: "Life for the Indian is one of harmony with Nature and the things which surround him. The Indian tried to fit in with Nature and to understand, not to conquer and to rule. We were rewarded by learning much that the white man will never know" (Standing Bear, 2006, 13).

Traditional teachers of the young people included tribal elders, grandparents and other relatives, parents, singers, and storytellers. Although education was not institution-based or literate like European American educational practices, scholars have documented that the subject areas covered in a traditional aboriginal education included biology, botany, geology, religion, literature, dance, art, music, astronomy, agriculture, mathematics, language, and government (Trafzer, 2006, 5). This learning was woven together with the acquisition of practical skills, such as farming, gathering, hunting, fishing, food preparation, and home- and community-building, equipping young people with both the knowledge and skill to survive and thrive in their society and environment. For traditional learners, the ultimate test was survival. Could a young person live off the land and thrive, after she/he was finished with "school"?

Given this view of education, it is perhaps not surprising that once the Native American tribes were overrun, defeated, and confined to reservations by the European American newcomers, that some elders were actually receptive to the idea of Anglo American education. Might not the education of the newcomers better equip their children for survival in this new, drastically changed world?

Meanwhile, the colonists undertook the education of the native inhabitants via religion, with their primary focus being conversion to Christianity. Religion and education were inexorably linked, and some early colonial educational experiences provided the foundation for the later boarding school era. In the next century, the educational efforts of the colonists continued under the auspices of religious missions, with the fledgling U.S. government contracting this service to the various religious denominations, who set up missions in the frontier areas. Given their remote locations, the missions also operated as boarding schools and were precursors to the government's boarding schools.

The government-run boarding school era officially began in 1879 with the opening of Carlisle Indian School, an experimental off-reservation boarding school for Native Americans started by Colonel Richard Pratt. Its perceived success spawned a series of boarding schools scattered throughout the nation, which continued through World War II and beyond. The underlying purpose of the government-run boarding schools was not education per se, but the assimilation of the Native American students into the larger European American society in the United States by means of a forced replacement of language and culture through immersion.

By now, tribal elders were not in agreement as to the value of the education for which they traded their lands so dearly in treaty documents. If these institutions provided an education that equipped their youths for successful future lives in the "new" America, it was more by accident than design. The boarding schools were often unwholesome places where diseases spread quickly and too many students died. Conditions were often harsh, with physical punishment a daily reality that was heretofore unknown to most Native American youths. And when the students returned home, they often were ill-equipped to deal with the reality of life on the reservation and often were uncomfortable with their traditional lifestyle, having become accustomed to boarding school conditions. Sometimes the returned students rejected their families and former lifestyles; sometimes their families found them so changed that they rejected the boarding school students. Often the students simply shed the superficial veneer of "civilization," like a snake shedding its skin, and returned to their former lifestyles, leaving their sojourn at boarding school behind them like a bad dream.

And yet, some students were able to take with them some elements from boarding school worth keeping and use them in their lives back home. They were able to create stories about their time in boarding school as a way to deal with this otherworldly experience and incorporate it into their lives. They became translators for the elders, the new generation of tribal chiefs, and the clerks and government employees at the local Indian agency. They became the teachers and maintenance workers at the boarding schools. They became political leaders, speakers, writers, and actors. They taught each other what it meant to be an Indian in the United States of America and created a new pan-Indian movement, which led Native Americans away from an existence as government wards and toward a new era of self-determination. The tribes could not have accomplished this individually, but the strength and solidarity of a pan-Indian movement achieved this goal for all Native Americans. One of the outcomes of the Native American self-determination movement was to take back control of their youths' education. Tribally run schools are a growing phenomenon, a testament to self-determination.

And the old boarding schools? As early as the 1930s, the U.S. government began shutting them down, as public schooling became available to Native American children. However, the Great Depression extended the lives of the remaining boarding schools, because they became a place of last resort for Native American families in poverty to have their children educated and cared for. After World War II, few boarding schools remained open, and those that survived did so only because of Native American support. By the end of the 20th century, the boarding schools had become residential high schools with a special curriculum emphasizing Native American language and culture, rather than seeking to eliminate it.

The story of Native American boarding schools is a story of change over time, and a history of the immense courage, creativity, and heart of the thousands of boarding school students who each crafted their own unique story out of a boarding school experience.

References

Standing Bear, Luther. *My Indian Boyhood.* New ed. Lincoln: University of Nebraska Press, 2006.

Trafzer, Clifford E. *Boarding School Blues: Revisiting American Indian Educational Experiences.* Lincoln: University of Nebraska Press, 2006.

Chronology

1606 Virginia Colony charter signed by King James of England. In it, he exhorts the colonists to convert the Indians to Christianity.

1629 Massachusetts Bay Colony chartered.

1656 Indian College Building built at Harvard University.

1659 Bible translated into Massachuset dialect and printed at Harvard University.

1665 Caleb Cheeshahteaumauk graduates from Harvard, the only early Native American to do so.

1675 King Philip's War and retaliatory massacre by colonists ends the praying towns.

1693 College of William and Mary established in Virginia, with American Indian educational mission.

Early 1700s The Great Awakening takes place; an evangelical Christian movement sweeps the American colonies.

1759 Samson Occom, a Mohegan, is ordained as a Christian minister.

1774 Occom's book published in English; first American Indian to publish in English.

1775–1783 American Revolutionary War—the colonies break ties with England and establish a new country, the United States of America.

1790s The Second Great Awakening sweeps the colonies.

1817 Brainerd Mission School established near present-day Chattanooga, TN, on Cherokee land; also, Foreign Mission School established in Cornwall, CT, the same year.

1819 U.S. Congress passes the Indian Civilization Fund Act in order to fund denominational missions for the purpose of educating and converting American Indians to Christianity.

Late 1820s   Policy of Indian removal established; East Coast Native Americans are forced to relocate to western lands.

1826   Elias Boudinot, a Cherokee, marries Harriet Gold.

1840s   California gold fever; increased westward migration by settlers, colonists, and gold seekers.

1851   Treaty of Fort Laramie signed by Sioux, Cheyenne, Arapaho, and 10,000 warriors; the majority of Native American tribes have been subdued by the American military.

1869   Grant's Peace Policy established.

1871   Congress establishes relationship with Indians as "wards of the government."

1877   Congress begins appropriations for Indian education.

1879   Carlisle Indian School opens in Pennsylvania.

1883   Indian Rights Association established.

1884   Haskell Institute opens in Kansas; Chilocco Indian School opens in Oklahoma.

1887   The Dawes Allotment Act is passed.

1891   Phoenix Indian School opens in Arizona.

1893   Pipestone Indian School opens in Minnesota.

1898   Estelle Reel appointed superintendent of Indian Schools; creates the Uniform Course of Study for the Native American boarding schools.

1900   Zitkala-Sa (Gertrude Bonnin) publishes articles about her boarding school and other life experiences in *Atlantic Monthly* magazine.

1911   Society of American Indians (SAI), the first pan-Indian national society, is formed.

1914–1919   World War I.

1918   Carlisle Indian School closes; national influenza epidemic affects boarding school students heavily.

1924   Citizenship granted to all Native Americans living in the United States; Essie Burnett Horne starts attending Haskell Indian Boarding School.

1925   Seven off-reservation boarding schools close. Boarding school enrollment is 8,542, the lowest ever. Native American students enrolling in public schools in large numbers.

1927 Curtis Carr begins attending Chilocco.

1928 Meriam Report criticizes boarding school conditions; National Council of American Indians (NCAI) established by Zitkala-Sa (Gertrude Bonnin).

1929 All BIA boarding schools are ordered to dismantle jails and cease using confinement as a punishment; corporal (physical) punishment is also forbidden in the boarding schools.

1929–1939 Great Depression; the worst economic era in the United States, plunged a large percentage of Native Americans into dire poverty.

1931 Luther Standing Bear's memoirs published.

1933 John Collier appointed commissioner of Indian Affairs.

1934 Indian Reorganization Act ends allotment.

1934 Johnson-O'Malley Act allows American Indian students to attend local public schools at federal expense.

1935 Adam Fortunate Eagle begins attending Pipestone Indian boarding school in Minnesota.

1939–1945 World War II.

1940 Lawney Reyes begins attending Chemawa in Oregon.

1953 Pipestone closes.

1960 Phoenix becomes Phoenix Indian High School.

1965 Haskell changes from a high school into a trade school.

1966 Rough Rock Community School (first tribally controlled school) opens on Navajo reservation in Arizona.

1968 Navajo Community College (now Diné College) opens at Tsaile, Arizona. It is the first tribally controlled college.

1969 Kennedy Report.

1970 Haskell becomes Haskell Indian Junior College; Chemawa avoids closure due to Native American support and a new campus is built.

1971 Southwest Indian Polytechnic University opens in Albuquerque, New Mexico; it is a tribally controlled college.

1972 Indian Education Act passed by U.S. Congress.

1972 Rock Point Community School moves from federal to local control on the Navajo reservation.

1980   Chilocco closes.

1990   Phoenix Indian High School closes.

1990   Native American Languages Act passed by U.S. Congress.

1991   Indian Nations at Risk Task Force Report.

1992   White House Conference on Indian Education.

1993   Haskell becomes Haskell Indian Nations University.

2000   The Bureau of Indian Affairs (BIA) operates 65 schools; the tribes operate 120 schools.

2010   Chemawa Indian School celebrates its 130th birthday.

ONE

American Colonial Period

DURING THE AMERICAN COLONIAL PERIOD, the main focus of the colonists was survival in a new, bewildering, and inhospitable land. Different colonies were established under different charters and were governed by proxy from afar, often by different governments in different countries. At this point, there were no established relationships with the native inhabitants in the colonies, and interactions between the colonists and the American Indians fluctuated rapidly between uneasy truces and violent bloodshed. The American colonists struggled to establish their own settlements and schools and were not overly concerned with the natives, who were far more adept at making a living on the continent.

However, most of the God-fearing colonists were convinced that their new neighbors were heathens, and it was their duty to Christianize them. Thus, education of the American Indians by the colonial interlopers began. In order to share the word of God, the colonists needed to communicate with the American Indians, which meant teaching them English. Once they began teaching the English language, reading, and writing, the rest naturally followed. Also, the cash-strapped colonists quickly discovered on their fund-raising trips to England that the British were much more likely to open their wallets to fund a mission to educate the American Indians than to build a school for the colonists' children. Indeed, such early institutions of higher education as Dartmouth and Harvard received much-needed cash infusions from the British in order to establish programs specifically for the Native Americans, which ultimately benefited very few of them but certainly helped the colonists.

During the colonial period, the lack of an on-site, centralized government ensured that any progress made in educating Native Americans was due primarily to the efforts of inspired individuals. The nature of the education offered to the local Indians was steeped in Christianity, as were most

1

of the educational efforts in the colonies at large. There was no particular policy, but the educational institutions that arose presaged the boarding schools that were established more than a century later. There were also independent efforts in the various American colonies to civilize and Christianize the Native Americans.

The Virginia Colony

The charter of the Virginia colony, signed by King James in 1606, exhorted the colonists to Christianize the Indians. The colonists came into contact with dozens of different Algonquian tribes, loosely categorized as the Tidewater Indians, as well as the Cherokees. During this period, Powhatan came to power as a leader among all of the Tidewater tribes, and their internal organization, lifestyle, and culture were at their peak. The colonists admired their abilities to subsist so well in the low-lying, swampy river and shore area they called Virginia. Unfortunately, the colonists themselves were not trained or prepared to make a living in the new land, and the local Indians saw nothing in the new colonists' culture or lifestyle that interested or appealed to them. Missionary efforts in Virginia were unenthusiastic, and the few efforts made to take selected Indian children into the colonists' homes to be educated were greeted with an equal lack of enthusiasm by the native Virginians.

One of the few documented education and conversion success stories to come out of the Virginia colony was that of Pocahontas, the daughter of Powhatan and the wife of John Rolfe. From 1616 to 1617, the Rolfes, with their son Thomas, and several other Algonquian children who were sent to England to be educated, lived at the British court. There, Pocahontas, or Lady Rebecca, as she was called in England, proved to be quite popular among the English courtiers. Many historians speculate that Pocahontas's popularity, and tragic death in 1617, led to the founding of Henrico College in Virginia. The economically strapped colony began building Henrico College in 1619, specifically to educate the local Indian populace. This effort was quickly brought to a halt by an Indian uprising in 1622, led by Powhatan's successor, Opechancanough, which resulted in the deaths of a quarter of the colonists. Instead of conversion and education, the immigrant Virginians went to war against the Indians in 1676 and ultimately reduced the colony's Indian population to less than 1,000.

Virginia's second chance to educate the local native populace occurred when Reverend James Blair, a Scottish clergyman, traveled to England in 1691 to obtain a charter for the College of William and Mary. He was suc-

Pocahontas (1595–1617) was one of the earliest Native Americans to experience an Anglo-American education. She was schooled in England, where this engraving was published in 1618. (Library of Congress)

cessful, and the college opened in 1693 to educate both the colonists' children and the Native American children. As the College of William and Mary identified ongoing funds for financial support of the Native American students and made it a condition of treaties with local native groups that some children must be sent to the College of William and Mary to be educated and to serve as hostages to the treaty, the college prospered, and its native student population grew. In 1723 a separate building, called the Brafferton, was constructed to house the Indian School and its students. There, the Native American students were instructed in the catechism of the Church of England, reading, writing, and arithmetic. They dressed like the colonial students and were instructed in English. Once they graduated, the thought was that they would go forth among their own tribes and convert other Native Americans to Christianity. In reality, this almost never happened; in fact, in one treaty conference recorded by Benjamin Franklin between the Iroquois and the Virginia colonial government, the Iroquois refused the offer of a colonial education for their children, because they said that the children thus educated who returned to the tribe "were absolutely good for nothing being neither acquainted with the true methods of killing deer, catching Beaver or surprizing [*sic*] an enemy" (Szasz, 1988, 77). They went on to politely offer an excellent and proper education to any English youths sent to Onondago (New York) by their parents to reside with the Iroquois.

In 1776, during the first year of the American Revolution, the British funding that supported the Native American students at the College of William and Mary ceased, and the students left the college. For 75 years, the College of William and Mary continued to educate young Native American men in the most lasting of the colonial educational efforts.

The Puritans and the Indians

The Massachusetts Bay Colony, chartered in 1629, depicted in its seal the conversion of the aboriginals to the Christian faith as one of its goals. Despite this mission, the colonists were slow to act on this charge; it was difficult enough to survive in the new land themselves, without worrying about the souls of the Native Americans. However, their presence proved useful when the Puritans sent Reverends Thomas Weld and Hugh Peter back to England to plead for funds for the new colony. They sought funding for the missionaries working with the Native Americans and for their fledgling Harvard College, established in 1636 to educate not only the colonial students but the Indian youths as well. In 1649, Weld and Peter's successor obtained a guarantee of ongoing financial aid to the colony's missionaries from England's Parliament, and the New England Company was established to disburse the plentiful contributions to the entire northeastern area of the New World for missionary efforts with the Indians. An Indian College building was also constructed at Harvard in 1656, but since there were no Native American students enrolled at the time, it was used to educate the local colonial students and to house the printing press that produced John Eliot's translation of the Bible into the Massachuset dialect between 1659 and 1663. Eliot was assisted by a number of natives who acted as translators and oversaw the printing of the Bibles. Only four or five native students ever studied in Harvard's Indian College, and only one, Caleb Cheeshahteaumauk, graduated (1665), only to die of tuberculosis soon after his graduation.

Although this pumped some much-needed funding into the northeastern colonies, the resulting success of the missionary efforts remains doubtful. For one thing, despite the ongoing funding, the number of devout Puritans willing to devote themselves to such missionary work was low. The successful missionary efforts during this time were spearheaded by a few individuals and their families. Even though they trained some of their native converts to carry on their work, this strategy also had limited success.

The Puritan colony had more success than the Virginia colony with Native American conversions, primarily due to Reverend Eliot. After his arrival in the New World, he furthered this effort by founding 14 praying towns with an estimated 1,111 Christian native inhabitants. The purpose of the praying towns was to gather together the Native Americans in order to teach them Christianity and a Christian lifestyle. Men were required to cut their hair; all inhabitants wore European clothing and learned to wash and prepare food in the European manner. Each town had a school with a Native American teacher, approved by Eliot. The teachers earned less than the missionaries, and the Native Americans earned less than the colonials. Eliot learned the native language from a Montauk named Cockenoe, who also helped him with his scripture translations. He ultimately published approximately 20 books in the Algonquian language, including the Bible, thanks in great part to the efforts of Cockenoe, and once he left to pursue his own career as an interpreter, his successor, Job Nesuton, a Massachuset. In his new career, Cockenoe, who could read and write, helped the Montauk defend their ownership of Shelter Island from colonial claims. Later, both Eliot and Nesuton were assisted by a young Nipmuc named Wowaus, who became James Printer after he completed his schooling and apprenticeship as a printer. Unfortunately, very few of the inhabitants of the praying towns could actually read or write, either in their own language or in English. Ultimately, fewer than 20 percent of the praying town inhabitants were baptized, including the Massachuset leader Metacom, known to the English settlers as Philip. King Philip's War, which began in 1675, ended the Puritan missionary efforts. The natives attacked the English, killing approximately 2,000 people in 25 villages. The English retaliated and killed more than 7,000 Native Americans and decimated the area. Most of Eliot's praying towns were destroyed, along with the Algonquian-language books. James Printer allied himself with King Philip but was able to return to his position as Eliot's printer after the war to reprint the lost books.

Another well-known missionary, Thomas Mayhew, established himself among the Wampanoag on Martha's Vineyard. For five generations the Mayhews worked with the local Native Americans. Like Eliot, Mayhew's success was largely due to a young Pawkunnakut, Hiacoomes, who became his interpreter and assistant. After his conversion, Hiacoomes continued as a minister and was most effective in Christianizing the local natives. Unlike Eliot's praying towns, the converted Wampanoags were not required to gather in special villages or give up their material culture. Mayhew established a school for the children and continued his ministry; both were quite successful and continued long after the praying towns disappeared on the mainland.

The 18th Century: The Great Awakening

During the 18th century, the Great Awakening swept the colonies, and emotional fire-and-brimstone preaching sparked a new interest in religion. Yale-educated Eleazar Wheelock was one of the popular itinerant evangelical Christian preachers of the day but soon settled down in Lebanon, Connecticut, to his ministry. Samson Occom, a Mohegan, was converted during the Great Awakening, and came to Lebanon to learn to read in 1743. At the time, he was 20 years old and a Mohegan councillor. Related to tribal leaders, he was already a person of significance among his own people. Intending to stay a few weeks, he ended up studying with Wheelock for four years. During that time he learned English, Latin, Greek, and Hebrew, and also began work as an itinerant preacher to Native American people. Ordained as a minister in 1759, Occom sought a teaching position to support himself, and went to Long Island, New York, to serve as a teacher and minister to the Montauk, and where he married a local woman and raised six children. Occom's brilliance as a student encouraged Wheelock to found an Indian school, Moor's Charity School in Lebanon.

Samson Occom was the first Native American to write and publish in the English language. He worked as a Christian minister and schoolmaster, and helped raise the funds that were used to found Dartmouth College. (Hill, William Carroll. *Dartmouth Traditions*. Hanover: The Dartmouth Press, 1902)

Wheelock believed that the Indian children should be removed from their homes and live at school. In a curriculum that foreshadowed Colonel Richard H. Pratt's boarding school established in the following century, Wheelock spent part of the day on studies and part of the day teaching the students useful occupations, to the disgruntlement of some of their parents, who felt that if their children were working on chores, they could better do this work at home. Wheelock's school educated many key Native Americans during colonial times, and served as a model for other Indian schools established throughout the colonies prior to the American Revolution.

Samson Occom was the first Native American to publish in the English language. Author of *A Choice Collection of Hymns and Spiritual Songs* (1774) and other works, he became disillusioned with Wheelock later in life, even though he remained Wheelock's ideal of a Native American student and his inspiration. Occom was bitter that he was paid less than the white colonials for the same missionary work among the Indians.

> Now you See what difference they made between me and other missionaries; they gave me 180 Pounds for 12 years of Service, which they gave for one years Services in another Mission.—In my Service (I speak like a fool, but I am Constrained) I was my own Interpreter. I was both a School master and Minister to the Indians, yea I was their Ear, Eye & Hand, as Well as Mouth. I leave it with the World, as wicked as it is, to Judge, whether I ought not to have had half as much, they gave a young man Just mentioned which would have been but [50 pounds] a year; . . . what can be the Reason that they used me after this manner? (Peyer, 2007, 47)

In 1766, Wheelock convinced Occom to travel to England to ask for funds for Indian education. Occom raised more than 11,000 British pounds, which Wheelock used to establish Dartmouth College. Occom became disgruntled with his mentor when he realized that the white students at the college far outnumbered the Indian students and that the funds he raised benefited very few Native Americans. He distanced himself from Wheelock because of his need to make a living and support his own family, struggling to compete with white missionaries. In the 1780s, he joined a movement to purchase land from the Oneida Indians and establish the Brothertown Indian Nation, a community of Christian Mohegan and Pequot Indians near Waterville, New York.

Wheelock continued to try to establish boarding schools, which he found far superior to community schools. When the Indian children attended community schools, they never attended on a regular basis and continued to be too much under the influence of their parents. The missionary thought that the children needed to be removed from their home environment and placed in a European environment in order to effect the proper change. However, he also believed that the best schoolmasters in the native communities were his Native American graduates, observing that they not only spoke the language but had more influence in the community than the European missionaries.

Southeastern Colonies

The Carolinas and Georgia were a different sort of area, inhabited by different colonists, and few educational efforts were established with the local Native Americans. With Charles Town as the major port for exporting furs, it was an area populated by hunters and traders. The rich soil drew planters and plantation owners, and their use of slaves began early. The traders sought to use the Native American hunters, who they generally cheated, to provide furs for the flourishing fur trade; local Indians were also in danger of being enslaved as plantation workers. Poor relations existed among the indigenous people and the colonists, punctuated by outright warfare. Most of the missionaries operating in the area were under the auspices of the Society for the Propagation of the Gospel (SPG) and lived close to the developed areas, afraid to establish missions in the wilderness. They ended up informally instructing a small number of Native American youths who happened to live near the developed areas and who came for day schooling and returned to their homes each night. There is very little documentation on the effects of this informal, low-key schooling and how it operated to the benefit or detriment of the youths involved.

One known story involves the son of the chief of the Yamasee people, referred to as the Yamasee Prince, who connected with Commissary Johnston in the Carolinas, who had him tutored and took him with his own family back to England to continue his schooling. Although not as famous as Pocahontas, he became known as Prince George and was able to master the English language and change his dress and living habits. After two years, he begged to return home, but the political situation had changed radically. The Carolinians and the Yamasee people were now enemies, and Prince George's father was defeated and sold into slavery upon George's return; no documentation exists about whether they saw each other again or how Prince George's life was affected after Johnston, with whom he lived, drowned. The fine education and transformation left the chief's son isolated and adrift in a quickly changing environment, with no anchor and no way home again. It is a tragic story.

Other Missionary Efforts

Although Wheelock's Indian school and his successful students, such as the Reverend Samuel Occom, were key figures in prerevolutionary America, there were other missionary efforts in the Middle Colonies and on the frontier during the 1730s and 1740s that promoted the combination of education and Christianization, which went hand in hand. These efforts were also inspired by the Great Awakening and included the German-speaking, pacifist Moravians, who were influential on the western frontier of what is now New York and Pennsylvania. The Moravians believed in what was called total immersion; the Indians were not only required to convert but to also change every aspect of their lives. They lived in European American settlements that were similar to Eliot's praying towns, where they lived in houses, went to market and church, and educated their children in local schools according to European American customs.

Educational Philosophy

The scholar Tsianina Lomawaima stated that the educational system imposed upon the Native Americans by the colonists had four basic tenets: Native Americans were savages and had to be civilized; civilization required Christian conversion; civilization required subordination of native communities, frequently achieved through resettlement; and civilization required special pedagogical practices to overcome assumed deficiencies. These hallmarks were included in all of the efforts to reculture and reeducate the indigenous populations that the European colonists came into contact with. This had to do with power; the colonists sought to eliminate native self-education, self-government, and culture and to establish control over these aspects by the colonists. These basic tenets continued throughout the history of Indian education by others and began to wane only in the era of self-determination, when Native Americans began to reclaim power over the education of their children.

Historians often address the issue of the success or failure of early colonial educational efforts among the Native Americans. The Europeans often viewed the results of their educational efforts as unsuccessful, because few Indian students actually were completely assimilated; that is, few converted to Christianity, lived European-type lives in American towns, and spoke English in their households. The persistence of Native American language and culture was viewed as a failure of the European American educational efforts. However, it is also true that several Native Americans learned enough of the English language and about the European American governmental system in order to become interpreters, cultural brokers, and advocates for their own people. Reverend Occom's role in a lawsuit regarding land owned by the Mohegans is not unique. Many of the European-educated Native Americans found themselves in leadership roles in negotiations with the colonists, advocating for their own people. Some also established their own communities, such as Brothertown, which were Christian communities comprised of Native Americans who controlled the culturally hybrid settlements to suit themselves.

The colonists' responses to the many Native American people in America veered from warfare and genocide to education and assimilation. The assumptions and tenets undergirding their educational programs for the American Indians continued throughout American educational history.

References

Butler, Jon. *Religion in Colonial America.* New York: Oxford University Press, 2000.

Lomawaima, Tsianina. "The Unnatural History of American Indian Education." In *Next Steps: Research and Practice to Advance Indian Education,* edited by Karen Gayton Swisher and John W. Tippeconnic, 1–31. (Washington, DC: ERIC, 1999).

Peyer, Bernd C., ed. *American Indian Nonfiction: An Anthology of Writings, 1760s–1930s.* Norman: University of Oklahoma Press, 2007.

Reyhner, Jon, and Jeanne Eder. *American Indian Education: A History.* Norman: University of Oklahoma Press, 2004.

Szasz, Margaret Connell. *Indian Education in the American Colonies, 1607–1783.* Albuquerque: University of New Mexico Press, 1988.

TWO

Missionary Educators: From Revolution to 1875—The Next Century

THE AMERICAN REVOLUTIONARY WAR (1775–1783) interrupted most of the Indian missions that received funding from England, and there were only a dozen or so missionaries working with the Native Americans by the end of the war. The new American government was anxious to have the local natives fight on their side, and if they had fought with the British, to establish peace with them afterward.

The young republic quickly created laws which allowed it to sign treaties with the Native Americans, the purpose of which was to allow the colonists to take over more and more land peacefully. The compensation offered to the Native Americans usually included a small amount of money and goods, as well as generous offers for Christianization and education, the two important and intertwined aspects of "civilization," that the European Americans found lacking in the native populace. Throughout much of the rest of the 19th century, the U.S. government negotiated nearly 400 treaties with various Native American groups, and most of them included the promise of education in return for relinquishing traditional lands.

There were also laws passed to control the unruly European American frontiersmen, who had primary contact with the Native American tribes and seemed to have established the unsavory habits of tricking, lying to, and cheating the Native Americans, as well as selling them alcoholic beverages. Such actions resulted in ongoing conflict that the new republic neither wanted nor needed. In 1792, President George Washington himself beseeched Congress to enact and enforce laws for the purpose of "restraining the commission of outrages upon the Indians" (Reyhner and Eder, 2004, 41). Unfortunately, this problem was never solved, not by George Washington nor any succeeding president. The frontiersmen as a group tended to be unethical, and bent on acquiring land through any means. They were lawless, by and large, ignoring the few laws set up to protect the

Native Americans, and stopped at nothing, including violence and murder, to get what they wanted.

One historian declares, "In the 1790s, no question was more pressing for the new national government than that of deciding the future status of Indians. In the main, the policy issue could be reduced to this fact: Indians possessed the land, and whites wanted the land. . . . The matter was an especially delicate one, for although the divestiture of Indian land was essential to the extension of American ideals, that divestiture must also be ultimately justified by those same ideals" (Adams, 1995, 5). Philosophically, the colonists believed their civilization to be superior to that of the aboriginal inhabitants, whom they classified as "savages." They noted that where the European-based settlements came into conjunction with the native settlements, the wild game hunted by the Native Americans disappeared, and theorized that the only way for the natives to survive was for them to take on the trappings of civilization, as their culture and way of life would inevitably give way to the superior European civilization. And if the natives could no longer make a living hunting the wildlife, they could turn to farming, and would need fewer lands in order to survive. Thus, the exchange of native lands for European education and civilization was rationalized.

The Second Great Awakening, which began in 1790, was responsible for most of the Protestant missions to the Native Americans during the next century. Although there was a lively debate among the missionaries whether civilizing or Christianizing the Indians should be the first step, it was an accepted fact that both were desirable and necessary. "Since conversion to Christ and civilization was conceived as an instructional problem, mission stations were educational establishments in the broadest sense" (Berkhofer, 1972, 15).

During these early years, the most difficult issue that the missionaries dealt with in both day schools and boarding schools was poor attendance by the Indian children. Some native parents did not value highly the mission schools, and if children were needed at home for economic reasons, such as hunting, planting, or harvesting, or if the family had seasonally nomadic habits, the children's school attendance suffered accordingly. Missionaries were not above using bribes to get the children to attend school; a warm building and a warm meal often inspired high attendance during the winter months. Missionaries also noted that those families that were habitually church-going or were of mixed-native parentage tended to have better attendance records. Indeed, even early missionaries found boarding schools to be more successful than day schools, because the free food, clothing, and board represented the largest lure of all.

One of the mission schoolteachers at the turn of the century described a typical school day, which began with prayers and reading scripture. Reading, writing, and math lessons were held until breakfast, after which was an hour of recreation. The children returned to their lessons until lunch and a two-hour playtime. Lessons commenced again until dusk, and the day ended with spelling lessons, hymn singing, and prayers. "Religion, as a survey of curriculums suggests, was an integral part of Indian education. For the greater part of the period under study, Bible and catechism were reading textbooks as in white schools. In both day and boarding schools, prayer and hymn singing were frequent, and attendance was required at Sabbath services" (Berkhofer, 1972, 31).

Indian Civilization Fund Act (1819)

In March 1819, the new republic of the United States of America formalized the exchange of civilization for lands in the Indian Civilization Fund Act, which established a federal contribution of $10,000 annually to be given to various denominational groups for the purpose of educating and civilizing the Indians. It has recently been observed by several scholars that this agreement ran counter to the separation of church and state that was so carefully crafted into the young republic's constitution. The fund was administered by Thomas L. McKenny, the first superintendent of Indian affairs. The act itself read that the funds are set aside to civilize the Native Americans "for the purpose of guarding against the further decline and final extinction of the Indian tribes" ("The Missionary Impulse"). This government subsidization of denominational schools established the norm for educating the native inhabitants, ostensibly for the betterment and continuation of the tribe. At the time, the European Americans foresaw only two possible outcomes for the native people, either destruction or assimilation into the dominant European American community. Although there were numerous diverse missions established among the Indians, the American Board of Commissioners for Foreign Missions (ABCFM), which was headquartered in New England, played a major role in this effort. An interdenominational agency created in 1810, the ABCFM supported overseas missions as well as in-country missions. More than half of their funds supported North American Indian missions, and the vast majority of their missionaries were Protestants from the Congregational and Presbyterian churches.

One missionary stated that his school's purpose was to teach "those habits of sobriety, cleanliness, economy, and industry, so essential to civilized life" (Quoted in Bowden, 1981, 168). Nineteenth-century missionaries all used similar methods to achieve their goals; they cut the children's hair, replaced native clothing with trousers, shirts, and dresses, and introduced soap, water, and combs. They gave the children new English names and taught them to eat with forks, sit in chairs, and perform household chores. They sought to change cultural concepts related to time, work ethic, and sex roles. Perhaps most life-changing was the replacement of the children's native language with English and introduction of the idea of private property (Bowden, 1981, 169).

The American Indians themselves reacted differently to the formal European-style education; some welcomed it and encouraged it, while others went to lengths to avoid this education. Early on, a division was created in many Native American societies; those who supported white education were "progressives," while those who opposed it were deemed "traditionals." This dichotomy continued throughout history.

Brainerd Mission School, 1817–1823

One example of a mission established by the ABCFM was the Brainerd Mission, established among the Cherokee Indians with their permission on the Chickamauga Creek, near what is today Chattanooga, Tennessee. The missionaries were New England Congregationalists, influenced by the Second Great Awakening and encouraged by the young U.S. government with its recently established Indian Civilization Fund Act. Cyrus Kingsbury established a mission at the Chickamauga site, supported by tribal leaders and mixed-blood Cherokees. He consulted with the secretary of war and received government approval and support for the creation of a manual labor boarding school, which was much more than just a church and a school. This school, like many others established during the Second Awakening, differed from the boarding school model pioneered by Wheelock in the previous century, which was based on exposure of the Native American students to a model missionary family. The students went to school and church and learned other domestic pursuits, so that they could in turn go out among other Native American communities as missionaries, in order to preach to the community, educate the young, and provide a model of civilized living, based on American Christian cultural values. Kingsbury's mission provided a model Christian *community* for the Native American students.

The mission flourished until 1838, just before the Cherokee removal, which forced all of the Cherokees off their land and onto the Trail of Tears. Those who survived their forced journey were relocated to the Oklahoma Territory.

The missionaries came to Chickamauga with the purpose of civilizing, educating, and Christianizing the Cherokee Indians. The Cherokees also had their own purposes for welcoming the mission. In their strong desire to retain their ancestral lands, the Cherokees welcomed education and Christianity, seeing it as a means by which they could establish equal footing with the European Americans. Alas, this was not to be. The deepest fears of the Cherokees were expressed eloquently by Principal Chief Pathkiller

The Brainerd Mission was a mission compound located on Cherokee land near present-day Chattanooga, Tennessee. In addition to a church and school, this self-sustaining settlement boasted gardens, fields, orchards, livestock, and a model Christian community. (Chattanooga Public Library)

in a conversation with the Brainerd missionaries, which was recorded in the school's journal:

> President Washington agreed where the line should be—had it run and marked—and told them this should always be the line between the Cherokees and white people—soon after there must be another treaty and another line—again another treaty and another line—and so on—always telling them this shall be the last line and always using the same reasons when they wished for more land. (Phillips and Phillips, 1998, 7)

Brainerd was larger than a school and a church. It was a small village; more than 100 people resided there, and more than 30 buildings were constructed to house all the mission's functions. The complex boasted a gristmill, sawmill, blacksmith, warehouses, barns, stables, fields, orchards, gardens, livestock, and a storeroom filled with cloth, notions, and school supplies. Kingsbury's model community "required a large number of laborers who exemplified Christian and civilized life in the controlled environment" (Berkhofer, 1963, 184). Although located in Cherokee country, another important attribute was that the school was isolated from the local tribal communities. "The institution was a self-contained community in the wilderness. The children were removed from their parents into a totally controlled environment" (Berkhofer, 1963, 184). After all, the goal of the missionaries was a complete cultural conversion, replacing their native culture with that of white, European, middle-class values. They wanted the children to be isolated and not contaminated by coming into contact with either their own community or with the white frontier community, which the pious missionaries deemed a harmful influence.

The school used the popular Lancastrian method of teaching, which the War Department promoted, since more students could be taught for less money. Spelling, writing, and arithmetic could be taught by older children acting as monitors to the younger children, when the children were divided by their abilities and taught systematically arranged subject matter according to their grade. Instead of textbooks, the children learned from printed cards, and they wrote in the sand or on a slate board. They were rewarded with a series of tickets and trinkets as they mastered their curriculum. In addition to learning "the common branches of knowledge," the students were also taught basic European American skills; the girls learned spinning, weaving, and other housewifely skills, and the boys learned how to farm and raise livestock.

Most of the missionaries worked earnestly to establish their mission and work within the Indian communities in order to educate and bring the gospel to their neighbors. The journal kept by the missionaries at Brainerd reveals their thoughts and opinions on a variety of subjects. When they arrived with the goal of Christianizing their community, they initially had no idea whether the Cherokees even knew of Christianity or opposed it. One missionary commented, soon after Brainerd was established, "there is nothing among this people to oppose the gospel, except their ignorance & the depravity of the human heart. They have not, as in the case with most heathen nations, a system of false religion, handed down from their fathers, which must be overturned in order to make way for the Gospel" (Phillips and Phillips, 1998, 51–52). Although the missionaries had a clear agenda and a righteous and condescending attitude toward the Native Americans they came to live among, they were definitely a better class of colonists than many the aborigines had previously met, since the majority of their interactions were with traders, whiskey sellers, and land-hungry backwoodsmen.

Indeed, the missionaries themselves expressed confusion about the contradictory policies toward the Indians that issued from the U.S. government. One Brainerd missionary wrote in the journal in 1818, "The Indians say they don't know how to understand their good Father the President. A few years ago he sent them a plough & a hoe—said it was not good for his red children to hunt, they must cultivate the earth. Now he tells them there is good hunting at the Arkansas; if they will go there he will give them rifles" (Phillips and Phillips, 1998, 60). This confusion marks a shift in U.S. policy; previously, the government had decided that educating and civilizing the Native Americans would allow them to live peacefully with their white neighbors. At the time, the new republic saw only two possible means for dealing with the Indians, and that was either to eradicate them or to assimilate them. The official policy became one of assimilation, which spawned the Indian Civilization Fund Act, and the support of numerous missionary societies by the government. However, the policy of assimilation, never terribly successful by anyone's standards, was slowly undergoing a change. Ostensibly to move threatened native groups out of harm's way, the U.S. government came up with the idea of trading traditional native lands for other lands further west, where, they figured, the Indians could live unmolested by the colonists who were rapidly populating the East Coast. This new policy of removal was shortsighted in many different ways; it assumed that lands were interchangeable and ignored the fact that most tribal cultures were built upon the peoples' relationship with their traditional lands, and it also neglected to factor in the insatiability of the

European American land hunger and the government's inability to control the westward movement of its people.

It is clear from the missionaries' journal that in addition to teaching the Cherokees, they learned something of the tribe and its language and customs while they lived at Brainerd. The entries often reflect knowledge and respect for their Indian neighbors, and they defend them to other American outsiders. One entry is in response to visitors who expressed surprise at the accomplishments of the children at the mission:

> We have reason to believe that the sentiment very generally prevails among the white people near the southern tribes, . . . that the Indian is by nature radically different from all other men, & that this difference presents an insurmountable barrier to his civilization. . . . We wish those who make the above objections to all endeavors to Christianize & civilize the Indians, might be reminded that the Indians are men; and their children, education alone excepted, like the children of other men. Considering the advantages of the children under our care, we think they are bright & promising as any children of equal number we ever saw collected. (Phillips and Phillips, 1998, 65–66)

In addition to teaching the Native American children, many mission schools, including Brainerd, educated African American children as well. As imperfect as the missionary schooling was, educational historians noted that in many rural areas, it was superior to the educational system established for the European American frontier children.

Foreign Mission School in Cornwall, Connecticut (1817–1826)

The enthusiasm and energy of the Second Great Awakening spawned numerous missions within the nationalistic United States in the wake of the War of 1812. Another example was the Foreign Mission School, founded in Cornwall, Connecticut, in 1816. It opened the following year with some Hawaiian students, then went on to educate about 100 youths from China, Greece, and the South Pacific, as well as American Indians, mostly Cherokees and Choctaws. Situated on the Housatonic River, the school was encompassed by a primarily agricultural community, with a small woolen factory and grain and lumber mills. The school's founders believed that the students would not only learn their lessons but would experience a perfect model community. In short, the town of Cornwall itself would provide a civilizing experience for the Native American students, giving them a model to emulate, and the townsfolk would be provided with a cautionary example of heathen manners.

Each school day included seven hours of study, work in the school's fields or wood lots, and mandatory church attendance. In addition to the basic curriculum, the students were taught astronomy, calculus, theology, geography, chemistry, navigation, surveying, French, German, Latin, blacksmithing, and coopering ("Foreign Mission School"). The school's excellent reputation soon attracted the sons of chiefs and other high-ranking Native Americans. Although the townsfolk enthusiastically cooperated with the school to "civilize" its students, they never accepted them as equals, no matter how closely their morals or manners resembled Cornwall's finest. Discrimination against the students was commonplace, and became obvious in 1825, when Elias Boudinot, a Cherokee student, asked for the hand in marriage of Harriet Gold, a daughter of one of Cornwall's leading citizens. Elias Boudinot was an exceptional student who graduated from a local school prior to attending the Foreign Mission School for four years and later the Andover Theological Academy. The previous year John Ridge, another Cherokee student, wedded Sarah Northrup, daughter of one of the school's trustees. However, the Boudinot proposal shocked the town, and both Elias and Harriet received death threats, and public demonstrations were held against their proposed union. Harriet was shunned and dismissed from the church choir and, fearing violence, fled from her home to stay elsewhere for awhile. Elias and Harriet were wed the following year and went to live in the Cherokee Nation in Georgia, where Elias went on to take a leading role and contribute to his tribe. Realizing the importance of literacy for the Cherokees, Elias partnered with Samuel Worcester upon his return to Georgia to found the tribe's first bilingual newspaper, the *Cherokee Phoenix*, which began publication in 1828 using Sequoyah's written version of the Cherokee language.

The negative public sentiment generated by the Boudinot marriage within Cornwall was turned against the school, which closed later that same year. The trustees were not unaware of the hypocrisy of their position. They promoted education at their school as a means to gain equality in European American society for Native American youths, and an outstanding student who conformed to all their ideals was rejected by the local community as being unworthy, simply because of his heritage. Not only did Boudinot surpass local standards of Christian civilization, he was a wealthy and important person in his own right. The trustees questioned the wisdom of pulling the students away from their homes and educating

Elias Boudinot (Cherokee) was a student at the Foreign Mission School in Cornwall, Connecticut, when he scandalized the town by courting and marrying Harriet Gold. He and his wife went to live in the Cherokee Nation in Georgia, where he began the first Native American newspaper, the *Cherokee Phoenix*. (Oklahoma Historical Society State Museum of History Collection)

them in Cornwall, and concluded that future mission schools should be situated in the areas where the students lived, such as Brainerd.

The Western Frontier

Due to the westward migration of the native tribes ahead of the encroaching Americans, and the increasing number of removals, where the U.S. government exchanged traditional tribal lands for other lands further west through treaty, the East Coast of the United States now held relatively few Native Americans. The native populations were still in the Midwest region and the western Plains, and the missionaries followed them westward. "By 1835, most tribes knew that the missionaries wanted to alter their culture with schools, agriculture, and Christian morals" (Bowden, 1981, 185). Repeated smallpox and cholera outbreaks further devastated and disorganized the native populations. Missions continued to be built on the western frontier, where the Catholics soon became as active as the Protestants. ABCFM still existed, and started the first missions to the eastern Dakota Indians during the 1830s.

Although the missionaries sought to completely replace the native spirituality with Christianity, and their own culture with the European American culture, they had already experienced some failure in replacing native languages with English. Although they continued to teach English to the children in the schools, their top priority was spreading the gospel and, as a result, much of their teaching was bilingual. The ABCFM was responsible for translating not only the Bible, but also elementary readers, catechisms, hymnals, and other moral stories into the Siouan language. As a part of this effort, they compiled and published a Dakota vocabulary, grammar, and dictionary. This was viewed as an effective method for making Christianity more accessible to the local people. In this manner, the early missionaries on the frontier pioneered the concept of bilingual education, a notion that became lost when the U.S. government entered the scene and began to establish government boarding schools.

Early Tribal-Run Schools

Tribally run schools did not begin in the 20th century. Some tribes had a history of establishing and supporting formal educational institutions. The Cherokee people, after their removal to Oklahoma, established their own governing body, the Cherokee National Council, which in turn set up a national school system with 11 schools. Initially staffed with missionary teachers, the schools, which were funded with the tribe's treaty dollars, gradually replaced the teachers with Cherokee instructors. The Cherokee Nation school system surpassed that of neighboring states in the 1850s, and even boasted male and female seminaries, which taught at the high school level.

Historians have noted that, even left alone, the Cherokee schools promoted Anglo-American education and lacked any sort of traditional curriculum to the extent that some full-blooded students attempted to burn down the seminary in protest. In spite of the fact that the Cherokee Nation was educating its students in a way that the government could not object to, and in higher-quality institutions at its own expense, the government sought to interfere, finding the Cherokee schools too academic, with not enough manual labor classes. This could indicate that the government was more interested in power and control than education and tried to establish the placement of Native Americans as second-class in the nation.

The Cherokees were not unique in their educational plans. The Creeks and Choctaws also established their own educational institutions after bluntly letting the missionaries know that they wanted their teachers, but not their preaching. Their schools also flourished in the 1800s, and the Choctaw system reported 84 schools operating in 1870, with primarily Choctaw instructors. These schools established by the tribes operated simultaneously with the missionary schools but were funded by the tribes themselves and received no encouragement or support from the federal government. The success of these endeavors preceded and predicted the era of educational self-determination in the 20th century.

Grant's Peace Policy, 1869

In an abrupt turnabout from the previous decades of rounding up Native American tribes, forcing treaty negotiations that inevitably resulted in the tribe being consigned to a small piece of land and the government owning vast new tracts (the alternative being death by U.S. military force), President Ulysses S. Grant signed into law his Peace Policy with the American Indians. The civilian Board of Indian Commissioners provided oversight for federal interactions with Indian tribes in an attempt to root out corrupt practices in Indian agencies. Also, churches were invited to nominate Indian agents to staff the agencies with high-minded, moral, Christian agents who would act as benevolent models as well as government agents. Ultimately, 13 religious denominations controlled 73 Indian agencies.

By the 1880s, the reform movement waned, as corruption in the Indian agencies was not significantly curbed, and a bitter rivalry was created among the various church denominations. The lack of cooperation and cohesiveness among the various denominations, combined with the success of a model government experimental boarding school in Carlisle, Pennsylvania, heralded yet another new direction for Native American education.

References

Adams, David Wallace. *Education for Extinction: American Indians and the Boarding School Experience, 1875–1928.* Lawrence: University Press of Kansas, 1995.

Andrew, John. "Educating the Heathen: The Foreign Mission School Controversy and American Ideals." *Journal of American Studies* 12, no. 3 (December 1978): 331–42.

Berkhofer, Robert. "Model Zions for the American Indian." *American Quarterly* 15, no. 2, Part 1 (summer 1963): 176–90.

Berkhofer, Robert. *Salvation and the Savage: An Analysis of Protestant Missions and American Indian Response, 1787–1862.* New York: Atheneum, 1972.

Bowden, Henry Warner. *American Indians and Christian Missions: Studies in Cultural Conflict.* Chicago: University of Chicago Press, 1981.

"Foreign Mission School." http://www.cornwallhistoricalsociety.org/foreign_mission_school.htm.

"The Missionary Impulse." *Digital History.* http://www.digitalhistory.uh.edu/native_voices/voices_display.cfm?id=45.

Phillips, Joyce B. and Paul Gary Phillips, eds. *The Brainerd Journal: A Mission to the Cherokees, 1817–1823.* Lincoln: University of Nebraska Press, 1998.

Reyhner, Jon, and Jeanne Eder. *American Indian Education: A History.* Norman: University of Oklahoma Press, 2004.

THREE

Carlisle Boarding School (1875–1900)

Beginnings

A YOUNG ARMY LIEUTENANT, influenced by his experiences with Native Americans on the frontier, came to fiercely believe in their intelligence and ability. It was his strong belief that the only thing standing between the first Americans and their full participation in the American society was education and their integration into the society at large. He decried the segregation resulting from the reservation system, and set about to reverse the direction of Indian education. In April 1875, Lt. Richard H. Pratt, 10th U.S. Cavalry, was assigned to escort 72 of the captured Indian leaders of a recent Indian uprising to the military prison at Fort Marion in St. Augustine, Florida, where they were to serve their sentences for murder and rape for an undetermined period of time.

Assigned as their jailor at Fort Marion, Pratt came to admire his charges and began to intercede with the authorities for clemency on their behalf. He was touched when Mah Mante, a Kiowa, asked to learn the white man's ways during his incarceration. Pratt began an experiment while at Fort Marion, finding work with the local souvenir dealers for his prisoners. The prisoners were able to earn money, and the scope of their useful employment expanded. In time, the prisoners milked cows, picked fruit, and guided local tourists on fishing trips, as well as working at other odd jobs. Pratt saw that the benefits of the prisoners having jobs included supporting the local economy, because they spent their money in town, they were kept occupied and out of trouble, and soon the prisoners adopted the dress and manners of the local white men in order to obtain and keep their jobs. Noting that communication remained a primary difficulty, Pratt persuaded other locals to come to the fort and teach English to the prisoners. Within a fairly short period of time, the irons had been completely removed from all prisoners, and Pratt had organized some of the younger prisoners into a quasi-military company and used them as guards. He had no disciplinary problems at the fort, and the amazing transformation of his Native American prisoners was the subject of approving articles in magazines and newspapers.

As a result, Pratt concluded that education was the answer to "the Indian problem," and he petitioned the government to provide a school for his prisoners as a next step. The War Department decided to send all of the Fort Marion prisoners back to their reservations instead, but the 22 youngest prisoners refused to return. Pratt sought private charitable donations to fund his 22 prisoners and wrote to many schools to procure places for them. All schools refused to take the Indians, with the exception of the Hampton Institute in Virginia. The Hampton Institute was originally established to provide basic education as well as agricultural and vocational training for the newly freed slaves after the Civil War. Once his former prisoners were established at Hampton, Pratt received orders to visit several tribes in the West and recruit additional Native American students for placement at Hampton Institute, and he returned with about 43 students from tribes near the Missouri River. But Pratt was unhappy because he was not in charge of the educational program the Indian students were receiving, and he believed that by being educated with African Americans, the Native Americans would become subject to the same prejudice and discrimination experienced by the Hampton students. In 1879 Pratt asked to be reassigned, and he decided to actively pursue his dream of establishing a school just for Indian students.

The Government's First Indian Boarding School

Pratt first identified a location for the school, which was an abandoned army barracks at Carlisle, Pennsylvania. Next, he had to persuade the government to give it to him for the purpose of establishing a new boarding school for Native Americans. In doing so, he needed to articulate his beliefs regarding Indian education, as they ran counter to the prevailing government philosophy, which supported mission-run, reservation-based schools for Native American children.

Through his successful experiment at Fort Marion, Pratt formulated the philosophy that informed his lifelong mission to educate the Native Americans. "In essence, his system consisted of taking the Indian out of his tribe and teaching him to speak, act, and think like a white man. That done, there would be no more Indian problem for the simple reason there would be no

Indian" (Morton, 1962, p. 60). In his zealous advocacy for Native American education, Pratt did not think deeply enough to realize the devastating and detrimental effects of the cultural genocide that he was promoting. He lobbied Secretary of the Interior Carl Schurz, who was appointed by President Rutherford B. Hayes in 1877. The Indian Bureau reported to Schurz, and in his career he sought to reduce the incompetence and corruption common in the Indian Bureau at that time. Later in his career, he created an Indian reform program. When they met, Pratt said to Schurz,

> You yourself, sir, are one of the very best examples of what we ought to do for the Indians. You immigrated to America as an individual to escape oppression in your own country. You came into fullest freedom in our country. You associated with our people, the best of them, and through these chances you became an American general during the Civil War, then a United States senator, and are now in the President's cabinet, one of the highest offices in the land. It would have been impossible for you to have accomplished your elevation if, when you came to the country, you had been reserved in any of the solid German communities we have permitted to grow up in some sections of America. The Indians need the chances of participation you have had and they will just as easily become useful citizens. (Pratt, 1964, 215)

With this argument, Pratt convinced Schurz to support his concept of an Indian boarding school in Carlisle, Pennsylvania. Pratt reasoned that since the government owned the property but wasn't using it, and it was not located in Indian Country, so that local white people would carry no prejudice against the Indian students, that it would provide the ideal location. The 27-acre compound contained numerous buildings that would initially provide all the necessary space for a boarding school. The order to give Carlisle to Pratt for his school was finally signed in 1882, and all the necessary approvals were won. Of course, Pratt had no funds to run the school and no students. Despite his enormous efforts, which resulted in victory, the hardest trials were yet to come.

Finding Students

Pratt was able to get funding through the same Indian Civilization Fund that supported the mission boarding schools on the reservations. Still, funding was never easy or plentiful, and the indefatigable Pratt used a variety of methods in order to keep his school operation solvent over the years. He continued to solicit funds from private and charitable sources, and ultimately managed to get military rations for the Carlisle students, which ensured that they were better fed than students at other boarding schools. But in the early days, his most difficult task by far was recruiting students.

Pratt needed to convince the vanquished chiefs of tribes that moved to reservations in the West to entrust their children to him in the East. This task was quite difficult because there was no force of law behind his appeal, and the chiefs had absolutely no reason to trust either Pratt or the U.S. government. To make things more impossible, the Indian Bureau required Pratt to enroll half of his new students from "troublesome" tribes, and stipulated that as many students as possible should be children of important chiefs. Government officials felt that the students would provide them with handy hostages if their tribes rose up and became hostile again.

Pratt was sent to Spotted Tail and Red Cloud, the Sioux chiefs who had just lost their beloved Black Hills. Pratt addressed the council, and they listened to him in silence. Then Spotted Tail stood and said, "The white people are all thieves and liars. We do not want our children to learn such things" (Pratt, 1964, 222). Pratt then addressed Spotted Tail personally. He told him that his lack of ability to read and write English, and his dependence upon interpreters, had led him to sign a treaty that he did not understand and that robbed the Sioux of their lands. He suggested that if the sons and daughters of the Sioux chiefs became educated, they could deal with the white men on even ground and stand up for their tribe. "Cannot you see it is far, far better for you to have your children educated and trained as our children are so that they can speak the English language, write letters, and do the things which bring to the white man such prosperity, and each of them be able to stand for their rights as the white man stands for his? Cannot you see that they will be of great value to you if after a few years they come back from school with the ability to read and write letters for you, interpret for you, and help look after your business affairs in Washington?" (Pratt, 1964, 223)

In the end, Pratt left with 66 children from the Rosebud reservation, bound on trains for Carlisle school. He also recruited students from Pine Ridge, and added some Kiowa, Comanche, Cheyenne, and Pawnee students, for a total of 136 students. Carlisle Indian School opened officially on November 1, 1879, with no staff, food, clothing, or equipment. Through Pratt's leadership and tenacity, Carlisle Indian School flourished and prospered.

Later boarding schools had an easier time recruiting students after a law was passed making schooling mandatory. At that time, students were forcibly removed from their parents' homes and taken to the nearest reservation boarding school. Nineteen Hopi men were imprisoned for a year

One of the common practices at Carlisle Indian Boarding School was to photograph the incoming students in their native garb, such as the unnamed students in this portrait taken around 1888. Later, the same students would be photographed again after they were dressed in school uniforms with regulation haircuts. This presented a bizarre before-and-after vignette meant to illustrate the civilizing influence of Carlisle Indian Boarding School. (Speck-Choate Photograph Collection, American Philosophical Society)

on Alcatraz for resisting school officials, and not allowing their children to attend Keams Canyon boarding school. Several Hopi memoirs allude to the practice of running and hiding as soon as the children saw school officials approaching the family hogan.

Student: Luther Standing Bear (Plenty Kill)

One of Pratt's first students recruited from the Rosebud reservation was young Luther Standing Bear (Plenty Kill), who later wrote several books in English about his life, experiences, and philosophy. His description of his trip back East and his subsequent experiences at Carlisle give a perspective from the Native American youth's point of view. He was not interested in the white man's education, but he knew that to go east to school was an act of bravery, and his focus in life at the time was to prove his bravery. He assumed he would go east, do something brave, and return to his home. Little did he realize that he would spend the next five years away from home; three years at Carlisle and the following two years working at a department store in Philadelphia. The 11-year-old boy who first entered Carlisle returned home as a 16-year-old young man.

In his memoirs, Luther Standing Bear relates that he was the first Indian to enter the Carlisle school grounds. "I had come to this school merely to show my people that I was brave enough to leave the reservation and go East, not knowing what it meant and not caring. When we first arrived at Carlisle, we had nothing to do. . . . We just ran all over the school grounds and did about as we pleased" (Standing Bear, 1975, 135). Eventually, the boys stuffed large bags with hay to be their beds, and teachers were recruited to teach the students. Luther tells of choosing a "white man's name" with a pointer and learning it as well as the English alphabet. One day, men came with large chairs, and the boys were called in one by one. All of their hair was cut off by the barbers. After seeing the other boys, Luther admits that he also wanted his hair cut off. "But when my hair was cut short, it hurt my feelings to such an extent that the tears came into my eyes" (Standing Bear, 1975, 141). Standing Bear tried very hard to reconcile his father's admonition to "be brave and get killed" with his new life at Carlisle. He relates how the boys were fascinated with the new western clothing they were given and paid rapt attention to their teachers, not to learn English, but to figure out how to put on the paper collar they were given, and to determine whether the opening in the pants went in the front or the back. They were allowed to choose their religious denomination, as Christianity and church became important parts of their new lives.

Luther Standing Bear (Lakota) was the first Native American student to enter Carlisle Indian Boarding School in 1875. This portrait was done later in his life; he went on to work at a trading post, act in movies, and write his memoirs in English, which were published in three volumes and are still in print today. (Library of Congress)

Upon arriving at Carlisle, the first group of students, including Luther Standing Bear, all had their hair cut off, were issued uniforms and English names. While Pratt and his teachers had practical reasons for all of these actions (i.e., their hair was cut to discourage lice and their new teachers could never remember their given names), the result was traumatic for the new students as the process of stripping away their cultural identities was begun. The children went to school for half a day and were instructed in a trade the other half of the day. Luther Standing Bear was instructed to become a tinsmith, a trade which was not useful on his reservation. He wanted to attend school the full day, as he thought to become his father's translator and bookkeeper (his father ran a trading post on his reservation). Instead, he was forced to learn how to make cheap tin cups, coffee pots, and buckets, which were sent to the reservations. Standing Bear jokes that there was no need for his services as a tinsmith, since the reservation had already received thousands of tin items created by the Carlisle students; however, his frustration at being forced to learn this useless manual trade after requesting a change is palpable in his written memoir.

He also relates how the students were taught music and formed into a band. During his first year, Standing Bear's father came to visit him at Carlisle. He was treated with respect by Colonel Pratt, who took him to visit the nearby cities and presented him with gifts. Luther was excited to see his father and proud of how he was treated and, encouraged by his father, redoubled his efforts to learn the ways of the Long Knives (white people), who, his father noted, were spreading over the land like ants and could not be defeated. During the summer months, many of the students were "outed"; that is, they were sent to live with local American families for the summer, boys helping with farm work and girls helping with house-work. The following year, Standing Bear and a few other students went back to the reservation to recruit more students for Carlisle. He recalls the continuing resistance of many of the Pine Ridge leaders to the idea of sending their children back East, since so many Sioux children became ill and died while at Carlisle. Standing Bear was able to address this issue and successfully returned to Carlisle with many new students.

At the end of three years, the first class was sent home, with the exception of Standing Bear and a few other students who wished to stay at Carlisle. He remained to further his education and work in a Philadelphia department store. Eventually, he returned to the reservation and worked for the agency, married and had children. For Luther Standing Bear, as for many of the children attending boarding school, his education was a mixture of experiences. There were things he liked and things he disliked about Carlisle. Although he was critical of some of the programs and people at Carlisle, he believed that the boarding school was a good idea and a benefit to him personally, although he admits in his memoir that given the choice of types of education, he would prefer to raise his own children with a traditional Indian education, rather than the American education.

The Arrival Experience

For most of the Native American students arriving at the off-reservation government boarding schools, their arrival and initial treatment were shocking, traumatic experiences that they remembered for the rest of their lives. There were certain common elements that students remembered about their starting at a government boarding school. Many of the children have memories of entering the school grounds through an archway, and being led into cold, dark, frightening buildings. "The entrance to nearly every Indian boarding school is marked by an arch, a symbol of the transition from 'uncivilized' space to 'civilized' space. As new students arrived at school and passed through the arch, they essentially passed from one life to another" (Archuleta, Child, and Lomawaima, 2000, 24).

Boarding school students were lined up, always standing in lines. They lined up for inoculations and health checks. They were issued government regulation clothing and were often required to discard all of their own clothing. Their hair was cut immediately and fine combed for lice. They lined up for baths. Family members were separated as the children were assigned dormitories based upon gender and age, with the beds in a line. They lined up for the mess hall, where they were served strange, unappetizing food, and they lined up early each morning for close-order marching drills, divided into companies. One Choctaw woman relates her memories of entering Chilocco boarding school for the first time: "At the beginning of every school year they inoculate you, and they lined us up just like you do in the Army, I used to say, like cattle, and I remember I had five inoculations. . . . And I was so homesick, and sick, I just thought I would die. That's one of the earliest things I remember. And another early memory was of being fine combed for lice" (Archuleta, Child, and Lomawaima, 2000, 25).

In an obvious effort to strip them of their culture and identity, students were not allowed to speak their native languages or practice any cultural traditions. Then they were given numbers or English names. More than one student compared their initial treatment at boarding schools as being similar to how animals are treated. Daklugie, an Apache from Geronimo's band, was sent to Carlisle along with other young Apache prisoners. He recalls his first days at Carlisle:

> The next day the torture began. The first thing they did was cut our hair. I had taken my knife from one of my long braids and wrapped it in my blankets, so I didn't lose it. But I lost my hair. And without it how would Ussen recognize me when I went to the Happy Place? The bath wasn't bad. We liked it, but not what followed. While we were bathing our breechclouts were taken, and we were ordered to put on trousers. We'd lost our hair and we'd lost our clothes; with the two we'd lost our identity as Indians. Greater punishment could hardly have been devised. That's what I thought till they marched us into a room and our interpreter ordered us to line up with our backs to a wall. I went to the head of the line because that's where a chief belongs. Then a man went down it. Starting with me he began: 'Asa, Benjamin, Charles, Daniel, Eli, Frank.' Frank was Mangus's son. So he became Frank Mangus and I became Asa Daklugie. We didn't know till later that they'd even imposed meaningless new names on us, along with the other degradations. I've always hated that name. It was forced on me as though I had been an animal. (Ball, 1980, 144)

Recollections of first days at boarding schools are often filled with resentment, anger, fright, and always homesickness. Whether they were at the boarding school from their own choice or because they had no other choice, they were children without their families for the first time, and they were all terribly homesick.

Gertrude Bonnin (Zitkala-Sa)

Although Carlisle was a unique experiment in that it modeled a government-run boarding school for Native American children, it flourished concurrently with the mission boarding schools. Zitkala-Sa, born Gertrude Simmons Bonnin, attended the White's Manual Labor Institute (a Quaker mission school) in Wabash, Indiana, and Earlham College, also in Indiana. She grew up to write about her experiences in boarding school and beyond, and eventually became a nationally known advocate for Indian rights in the United States and founded the National Council of American Indians in 1926, serving as its president until her death in 1938.

Unlike Luther Standing Bear, she found little to admire in her youthful boarding school experiences. Like many others, she was recruited by missionaries at the age of eight, because she wanted to go East with her friend back to a place where she could pick all of the red apples she desired. In her essay, "School Days," Zitkala-Sa describes how she ran and hid under a bed when she found out that the matrons intended to cut her hair, a common boarding school practice. "I remember being dragged out, though I resisted by kicking and scratching wildly. In spite of myself, I was carried downstairs and tied fast in a chair. I cried aloud, shaking my head all the while until I felt the cold blades of the scissors against my neck, and heard them gnaw off one of my thick braids. Then I lost my spirit" (Zitkala-Sa, 1985, 55–56).

Despite the difficulties she had adjusting to boarding school, Zitkala-Sa found herself also unable to fit in at home when she visited in the summers, and her estrangement from her very traditional mother continued throughout her life. After two years at Earlham College (1895–1897), she accepted a position at Carlisle as a teacher. In her *Atlantic Monthly* article, "An Indian Teacher Among Indians" (Zitkala-Sa, 1921), she reveals that many of her Caucasian colleagues were incompetent and interested only in occupying their positions as teachers at Carlisle as a means of steady income. Zitkala-Sa acknowledged that there were some of the teaching staff dedicated to their students, but that there existed a lack of oversight necessary to cull out the dead wood and make the school excellent. Colonel Pratt, no fan of the civil service system, would probably have agreed with her. During her tenure at Carlisle, she never made friends with her fellow teachers, but unfortunately she did not address her relationships with her students in her memoir. Pratt soon sent Zitkala-Sa back to her reservation to recruit more students. She took the opportunity to visit her mother, only to find they had become irretrievably estranged. After two years at Carlisle, she quit to pursue her own studies and interests.

Carlisle School Days

Most students attended Carlisle for three years, after which they returned home with a trade to begin work or further their education in a regular public school, if available. This led to an educational program unlike any other in the United States; half of Pratt's program was educational, but at a very basic level, because of the lack of English language skills among the students. The other half of the Carlisle program emphasized Carlisle's establishment as an industrial or trade school. Pratt chafed at this, fully aware that the students were being shortchanged educationally. He wanted to introduce the students to English as a second language, then mainstream the students into the public schools. He felt that they could attend high school and college with other American students, paying their own way by getting a job in a trade they learned at Carlisle. He ran into several roadblocks; neither the Native American parents nor the Washington bureaucrats were willing to let him have the children for more than three years at government expense. Thus, his awkward hybrid program was born in which many students learned some basic English and returned to the reservation schooled in an occupation such as agriculture, carpentry, shoemaking, printing, tinsmithing, or tailoring, many trades that proved useless back on the reservations, depending upon the individual student.

Those students who did continue their education in mainstream high schools and colleges found that their Carlisle education did not prepare them adequately to compete in the public schools, and they encountered strong resistance and prejudice from the local whites who did not share Pratt's conviction that the Native Americans were just as intelligent and

Carlisle Indian School students had a program that was half academic, half manual labor training. This academic classroom at Carlisle features students reading in class; reading and writing in English comprised the core academics, along with mathematics. (Library of Congress)

capable as the European American students. Some Native American students did achieve higher education through extraordinary dedication and effort, but many roadblocks were placed in their way. Many others returned to their reservations with enough knowledge of the English language to get a job in the reservation bureaucracy. True to Pratt's predictions, they became the cultural translators for their tribes, the link between their tribes and the U.S. government, and were able to provide the tribal members with a voice in their governance for the first time since they were confined onto reservations.

Those Native American students entering Carlisle who did not speak English were not given books, only slates and chalk, and class consisted of naming and writing names representing common objects. Classes continued with basic education; in 1889 Carlisle added a normal department for teaching teachers, after students graduated from the eighth grade. The normal department students helped teach the entering and younger students. The school had an elaborate print shop that produced a newspaper, *School News*, as well as the monthly *Red Man* and the weekly *Indian Helper*. These publications were in English and were used to promote Pratt's message of assimilation and for students to encourage each other to use English. Although the use of their native languages was officially prohibited while on campus, this was difficult to enforce and native language use did occur, based on the flow of articles in Carlisle's publications exhorting students to speak English at all times.

Although the educational program was very basic at Carlisle, the extras were not neglected. Carlisle had a music program with a 30-piece band. During 1892, the Carlisle students in their neat military uniforms, accompanied by their band and a large banner that read "Into Civilization and Citizenship" marched in parades in both Chicago and New York. Pratt was highly aware of the necessity of advertising his program and promoting it in a positive light in order to keep the government funds coming in. Like many other Indian educational programs, Carlisle's burgeoning fame rested primarily upon its sports programs, about which Colonel Pratt was quite ambivalent. Although he enjoyed the publicity they garnered, he was concerned about the violence of the sports, especially football, and thought this to be a negative influence on the student body. The students wanted to play sports, so Colonel Pratt hired the legendary "Pop" Warner as a football coach, and he created a winning team; one that traveled around the country playing and making money for Carlisle, and which produced such exemplary athletes as Jim Thorpe. There were other less well-known athletes that graduated from Carlisle and went on to higher education, and ended up coaching at U.S. schools.

Carlisle Outing Program

One of the hallmark programs that Colonel Pratt established at Carlisle and which was copied by other government boarding schools was what Pratt referred to as the "outing" program. For him, this embodied Carlisle's mission: "To civilize the Indian, get him into civilization. To keep him civilized, let him stay" (Pratt, 1964, 283). Pratt's idea was that students would leave the school during the summer vacation and live with an American family, doing paid work. In the case of the girls, it was primarily housekeeping, and the boys were employed doing farm work and other chores. Pratt set up bank accounts for each of his students, and their earnings accumulated. It was his hope that they would use their savings to fund their own higher education.

This program was quite popular with the locals, who got cheap labor for the price of room, board, and a token salary. As with the other Carlisle programs, the results were mixed. Some of the students were treated harshly as servants, and were poorly paid, if at all. Others were treated as family members and were paid equally with other hired help. Pratt's memoirs contain many letters from the hosts of the Carlisle students, praising their abilities and their outstanding characters. Even if the student's experience was nothing more than a summer job of paid drudgery, many outing hosts found themselves educated and their minds opened about Native Americans, as Pratt intended. He was most emphatic that the location of the school in Pennsylvania was central to the success of the outing program, citing the continuing hatred and prejudice of the western European Americans as a roadblock to congenial relations and successful integrated educational programs.

Health Issues

Currently, there is little left to remind us of the Carlisle Indian School, other than the shockingly large graveyard, filled with rows of similar white headstones bearing such names as Fanny Chargingshield, Dora Morning, and Samuel Flying Horse. The 186 headstones also list a tribe and a death date. Just as Carlisle provided a model for future government boarding schools for Native American youths, the pernicious health issues that plagued Carlisle continued to take too large a toll of student lives at all of the boarding schools. The students faced diseases that their immune systems were not prepared to handle. Brought to Pennsylvania from many different places, and confined in crowded dormitories, sharing meals in mess halls and sharing towels and musical instruments, it is no wonder that diseases swept through the student populations. In addition to periodic influenza outbreaks, the most common diseases in the boarding schools were trachoma, an infectious and painful eye disease, and, most especially, tuberculosis.

Tuberculosis continued as the number one killer of boarding school students for decades. The infectious nature of the disease was not understood until later, and it was thought at the turn of the century that the Native American students were more prone to the disease due to their physical inferiority and poor constitutions. In truth, the poor nutrition and unsanitary and crowded conditions that existed at all the boarding schools encouraged the spread of communicable diseases. Decades later, the Meriam report would castigate the boarding schools for their poor attention to health. Meanwhile, Native American students died by the hundreds. Students who came down with tuberculosis were often sent home to die, but the boarding school graveyards attest to the many who passed away while at school. Over the years, many boarding schools built their own hospital buildings on the grounds in order to accommodate sick students, especially after the infectious nature of disease was understood. In fact, the Phoenix Indian School hospital eventually served as a tuberculosis sanatorium for the surrounding Native American tribes, as this was a widespread disease among the population.

The other danger the students faced was widespread homesickness. The shock, fear, and loneliness that the students experienced upon arriving at the boarding schools and experiencing total institutionalization for the first time cannot be underestimated in terms of detrimental health effects. The psychological impact affected already challenged immune systems, and the homesick children ran away with heartbreaking regularity. Located far from home in Pennsylvania, runaway students ran the risk of death by exposure, which is how more than one student met his or her end. Other students became severely depressed, which may have led to physical illness or even suicide.

Probably the first grave dug at Carlisle was for Lucy Pretty Eagle, a Sioux called Take the Tail by her own people. She arrived with Luther Standing Bear and the first group of students from the Rosebud Reservation. She was dead within three months of unknown causes, buried at age 10 in a strange place, the first of many yet to follow. Perhaps it is fitting that ghost stories grew up about her in the area, and locals claim that she haunts the former Carlisle boarding school buildings.

The Carlisle Story

Carlisle started up in 1879 with 136 students. Colonel Pratt directed the school for 24 years, and graduated only 158 students during that time. The students who graduated and returned home probably had a fourth grade education and training in a trade that may have been useless at home. Pratt was a stern disciplinarian, but believed with all his heart that his Native American students could do anything that other American students could do, if given the proper education. Despite his refusal to see anything positive in native cultures, his firm belief in the power of education for Native Americans and the model of Carlisle infused American educational policy for years to come. In 1911, 509 of 574 living Carlisle graduates were employed, 209 in government jobs and 300 in the private sector (Reyhner and Eder, 2004, 147). Encouraged by Carlisle's apparent success, the U.S. Congress funded 23 more off-reservation boarding schools after 1879. These schools competed with the mission-run boarding schools on the reservations.

Colonel Pratt continued to be outspoken in his views. He despised the Indian Bureau and the Bureau of Ethnology, viewing them as unnecessary bureaucracies developed only to offer continued employment to incompetent Anglo-Americans. While there may have been some basis for this observation, he also wished to eradicate the study of native cultures, and saw these departments as glorifying and upholding native traditions that, to his way of thinking, should be eliminated and forgotten. Pratt butted heads with Theodore Roosevelt and was retired from service. He stayed on at Carlisle as an adviser but was finally dismissed in 1904 when he again called publicly for the termination of the Indian Bureau.

The Carlisle Model

The Carlisle model of off-reservation boarding school education for Native American children ran counter to many of the practices of the mission boarding schools, with which they competed for students. Once the government saw and approved of the Carlisle model, government funds were used to establish similar off-reservation boarding schools, although none was located so far east as Carlisle. Government funds began to dry up for mission-based schools located on reservations, although the privately funded mission schools often became elementary schools feeding into regional government boarding schools, which offered a high school curriculum. In the beginning of its existence, Carlisle's curriculum was a strange amalgam of English language learning, basic elementary school curriculum, and trade school. Pratt's trade school and outing experiments persisted in Native American education past the turn of the century. Although the European Americans had just defeated the native tribes in order to dominate the North American continent, Pratt was unique in seeing the defeated children as equal to all other American children in terms of intellect and capability. His program of immersing his students in American culture as if they were the children of new European immigrants was considered unusual at the time, but effective. Carlisle's problems of sickness, death, and runaway students were also endemic to the boarding school culture and persisted in other boarding school environments, along with the harsh suppression of students' cultural identities.

The reactions of the students were as varied as the students themselves. Luther Standing Bear appreciated some experiences he had as a student and how his Carlisle education helped his life after he returned home. He also experienced terror, homesickness, and disappointment that Carlisle was not a place for an educational exchange, but only for copying the white man. Educated at the same time at a different boarding school with a brief sojourn at Carlisle as a teacher, Zitkala-Sa experienced a deep divide in her life and was unable to return home or fit in with her family. Her experiences turned her into a reformer, who spent the rest of her life using her English writing skills to fight for Indian rights and citizenship in the United States. Other stories abound, and all are voices of the boarding school experience.

Carlisle became a model and an icon for boarding schools. In the government's quest to civilize the Indians, "boarding schools, especially the off-reservation variety, seemed ideally suited for this purpose. As the theory went, Indian children, once removed from the savage surroundings of the Indian camp and placed in the purified environment of an all-encompassing institution, would slowly learn to look, act, and eventually think like their white counterparts" (Adams, 1995, 335). Suffice it to say that whether one looks at graduation rates or at case studies, Carlisle and its counterparts failed to accomplish their purpose most of the time. This is not to say that the boarding school educational experience could be labeled as a complete and total failure; the outcomes were varied and simply not what the government expected to accomplish.

The End of Carlisle

In the late 19th century, Colonel Pratt's criticism of government support of Indian mission schools was only exceeded by his criticism of the Indian Bureau and of the government's civil service hiring system, which was extended to the off-reservation boarding schools. Pratt resented being told by the government who he could and could not hire to teach at Carlisle and expressed the same disgust as Zitkala-Sa that some teachers hired into the civil service system only put forth minimal effort to keep their salary coming and cared nothing for their students.

Pratt's enthusiastic embrace of complete assimilation as a policy for Native American education, once popular, was becoming less so, and his supporters decreased as his detractors increased. In 1904, he addressed the New York Minister's Conference, publicly advocating the destruction of the Indian Bureau, and was dismissed. After Pratt left Carlisle, he was replaced by one of the career bureaucrats he disliked so much, and the athletic program was emphasized to the detriment of the school. In 1913, the students petitioned the government to investigate conditions at the school, and corruption in the school's athletic program was exposed. Another new superintendent was appointed, who let discipline lapse, so that runaways and expulsion of pregnant girls became more common. Finally, using World War I needs as a pretext, Carlisle was closed forever in 1918 and returned to its original use as an army facility.

References

Adams, David Wallace. *Education for Extinction: American Indians and the Boarding School Experience, 1875–1928.* Lawrence: University Press of Kansas, 1995.

Archuleta, Margaret L., Brenda J. Child, and K. Tsianina Lomawaima, eds. *Away from Home: American Indian Boarding School Experiences, 1879–2000.* Phoenix, AZ: Heard Museum, 2000.

Ball, Eve. *Indeh: An Apache Odyssey.* Norman: University of Oklahoma Press, 1980.

Landis, Barbara C. "Putting Lucy Pretty Eagle to Rest." In *Boarding School Blues: Revisiting American Indian Educational Experiences*, edited by Clifford E. Trafzer, Jean A. Keller, and Lorene Sisquoc, 123–30. Lincoln: University of Nebraska Press, 2006.

Morton, Louis. "How the Indians Came to Carlisle." *Pennsylvania History* 29, no. 1 (January 1962): 53–73.

Pratt, Richard H. *Battlefield and Classroom: Four Decades with the American Indian, 1867–1904.* New Haven: Yale University Press, 1964.

Reyhner, Jon, and Jeanne Eder. *American Indian Education: A History.* Norman: University of Oklahoma Press, 2004.

Standing Bear, Luther. *My People, the Sioux.* New ed. Lincoln: University of Nebraska Press, 1975. Originally published Boston, New York: Houghton Mifflin, 1928.

Zitkala-Sa. *American Indian Stories.* Reprint. Lincoln: University of Nebraska Press, 1985. Originally published Washington: Hayworth Publishing, 1921.

FOUR

Haskell Institute (1900–1920s)

FIVE YEARS AFTER Carlisle opened its doors, the Haskell Institute (originally the United States Indian Industrial Training School) started up in Lawrence, Kansas (1884). Named for the Kansas legislator responsible for locating it in Lawrence, Dudley Chase Haskell, it was patterned after the Carlisle model and was a coeducational, off-reservation boarding school run in a military manner. In 1905, 70 staff members and 1,127 students lived at Haskell; by then it was the largest government Indian boarding school in the United States.

Historic Context: Turn of the Century

In 1887 the Dawes Allotment Act passed, which parceled out reservation lands held in common to individual family members, with each head of household receiving 160 acres, each single adult 80 acres, and each child 40 acres. In the post-treaty era, this act was responsible for the loss of more than 90 million acres of land by indigenous peoples in the United States between 1887 and 1933. Further massive land losses proved devastating to Native Americans who had already seen the vast majority of their traditional lands swept away by the government through peace treaties. By the turn of the century, the majority of Native American families lived in poverty. The Native Americans of the 20th century knew well what was happening, and where their best interests lay. Many adults and children saw education as the best path to a viable future, and the boarding schools required less forceful recruiting in order to fulfill their enrollments. Indigenous families began to view boarding school as a way to feed and clothe children while providing them with the education that would enable them to live lives better than their parents had.

Another social change that occurred in the new century was a change in the assimilationist reformer attitude that imbued Carlisle and other off-reservation boarding schools. The attitude that Native American children were equally capable as all American children, given the same education, was eroded in an era of scientific racism. Native Americans and other racial minorities were now seen as being less intelligent. Where Richard Pratt introduced training in the trades primarily as a means for the students to make money in order to continue their education, Estelle Reel's vision of Indian education was one based primarily on manual training, and as the newly appointed national superintendent of Indian schools, she had the political clout to implement her vision.

In the 1900s, a more cohesive vision of Indian education prevailed nationally, and the boarding schools were somewhat less of a hodge-podge of classes. During the previous decade, Commissioner of Indian Affairs Thomas Jefferson Morgan reenvisioned the place of off-reservation boarding schools in the educational continuum. The schools were organized so that primary education took place at the reservation schools, and the off-reservation boarding schools were responsible for secondary education, with students coming from the primary schools on the reservations. Haskell was to offer a curriculum consisting of English language training, academics, moral training, and industrial training. In addition, Haskell offered normal (teacher) training and business training, offering its students access to white collar professions, which other schools did not.

Daily Program at Haskell

Haskell's school calendar for 1919–1920 lists the following daily program for the weekdays, detailing the lives of its students from dawn to dusk:

5:30 A.M.	Rising bell and reveille
6:00 A.M.	Gymnasium and military drill
6:25 A.M.	Bugle; roll call
6:30 A.M.	Breakfast
7:00–8:00 A.M.	Band practice
7:00 A.M.	Clean up quarters (non-band members)
7:15 A.M.	Warning whistle for Industrial Dept.
7:30–8:00 A.M.	Industrial Dept. instruction
7:55 A.M.	Academic school bell
8:00 A.M.	Industrial Dept. production work begins
8:00 A.M.	Academic Dept. sessions begin

11:30 A.M.	Midday whistle
11:55 A.M.	Mess call; midday roll call
12:00 noon	Dinner
12:55 P.M.	Warning whistle for Industrial Dept.
1:05 P.M.	School bell
1:10 P.M.	Industrial and Academic sessions begin
4:10 P.M.	Academic Dept. closes
4:10 P.M.	Band practice
4:20–5:20 P.M.	Athletics for boys
4:00–5:30 P.M.	Gymnasium classes and bathing for girls
5:10 P.M.	Industrial Depts. close
5:50 P.M.	Mess call; roll call
6:00–6:30 P.M.	Supper
7:30–8:30 P.M.	Evening sessions
8:45 P.M.	Tattoo
9:00 P.M.	Call to quarters
9:15 PM	Taps

On Saturdays, after a half day of work, the students were allowed to visit town, boys and girls alternating. Sundays were set aside for church services, often followed by a dress parade or band concert (Vuckovic, 2008, 91–92).

One student who attended Haskell in the early 1920s, Esther Burnett, corroborates this schedule in her written memoir. "After morning drill we went to breakfast, which usually consisted of bread and corn syrup, peanut butter, oatmeal, cooked dried fruit, and a cereal beverage" (Horne, 1998, 35). She went on to say that after breakfast, the students had "detail," which consisted of cleaning the campus and doing chores. "Kid power" was used to care for farm animals, milk cows, and harvest vegetables, which kept the boarding school running, a state of affairs that was true throughout the U.S. Indian boarding school system. The funds allocated from the government and received from private donors were never enough to keep the schools functioning and to adequately feed and clothe all the students. So, under the guise of educational training, the boarding schools used their students as unpaid labor to keep farms, gardens, and bakeries running in order to supply all of the needs of the students and make the schools self-sufficient. "In 1928, when the secretary of the interior commissioned a study of the work of the Indian Service, per capita rates to fund schools were painfully low. Federal Indian schools received $225 per student per year. . . . Students baked pies, built and repaired buildings and furniture, washed and ironed laundry, fixed uniforms and shoes, ran power plants, milked cows, grew and harvested crops, ran printing presses, cleaned acres of buildings, and polished miles of corridors" (Archuleta, Child, and Lomawaima, 2000, 35). In many boarding schools, the abuse of this policy led to students being overworked in menial chores and their education and health suffered. Also, poor planning and mistakes often led to inadequate food supplies and mal-nourished children in the boarding schools.

Educational Policy, 1900–1927

In the 20th century, new policies reversed Pratt's educational policies for Native American children. Superintendent of Indian Schools Estelle Reel, appointed in 1898, emphasized the vocational training in Indian board-ing schools. She believed that the Native American children were intel-lectually inferior to European American children, and that the best use of government educational funds was to train them for their place in the greater American society. Her vision was that the Indians would fulfill their destinies as laborers, housekeepers, and craftsmen in America.

Reel also proposed the Uniform Course of Study in her 1901 annual re-port, so that all of the different institutions could be teaching the same courses at the same levels, and there would be less confusion for students transferring between institutions. Up until this point, there was little effort to ensure consistency among the various government boarding schools. Her outline covered 31 subjects and detailed what should be covered in each year of school for each subject. Her list of courses gives a complete picture of what the curricula of the boarding schools looked like, beginning in 1902: agriculture, arithmetic, the bakery, basketry, blacksmithing, can-ing, carpentry, cooking, dairying, engineering, the evening hour, gardening, geography, harness making, history, housekeeping, laundry, music, nature study, outing system, painting, physiology and hygiene, printing, reading, language and subprimary work, sewing, shoemaking, spelling, tailoring, upholstering, and writing.

Another new direction was established by Commissioner Francis E. Leupp, who supported incorporating native materials into the educational curriculum. Previously, Pratt had opposed allowing any Native customs, culture, or language to permeate the boarding school, feeling that stripping the boarding school students of their culture was a necessary component of their education. Indeed, this belief gave rise to the most horrific aspects of Native American boarding school education, such as the hair cutting, the discarding of clothing and objects from home, and the brutal suppression of native languages. Leupp stated in 1907, "I have none of the prejudice which

Haskell Institute adhered to Estelle Reel's uniform course of study, which standardized the curriculum across the Native American boarding schools. Here, male students learn carpentry in class during the early 1920s. (Library of Congress)

exists in many minds against the perpetuation of Indian music and other arts, customs, and traditions" (Adams, 1995, 316). Leupp went on to support a program at Haskell to improve English composition skills by describing local customs or retelling native stories in English. Many of these were published in the Haskell school newspaper, *The Indian Leader*, and in 1913, Haskell published a book, in English, containing Native American tales.

Leupp also encouraged schools to teach Native American arts and crafts, which required hiring native instructors. He saw it as another means of giving students skills that would allow their economic independence. Indeed, they were more likely to sell handcrafted rugs, baskets, pottery, and beadwork than the same tin cups and plates that could be purchased anywhere else. These changes made good sense but did not fundamentally alter the boarding school experience.

As early as 1907, Commissioner Leupp clarified the government's education cational vision for Native American children in the 20th century, establishing that most of the education for Native American children should take place on the reservation or in local public schools, and that off-reservation boarding schools should be limited in number and used only for higher education. He went on to suggest that the government should begin to shut down the off-reservation boarding schools. Between 1900 and 1925, 44 government schools were closed, including 7 off-reservation boarding schools. By 1925, student enrollment in off-reservation boarding schools stood at 8,542 students, the lowest enrollment since the turn of the century, and much less than the peak year of 1915, when 10,791 Native American students were enrolled in off-reservation boarding schools. During this period of time, the enrollments of Native American students in local public schools increased greatly, supported by government funding.

Reasons for Continued Boarding School Strength

Despite the change in direction, boarding schools continued to show strong enrollment for a number of reasons. Many Native American children still lived in areas of the country that were undeveloped and remote; there were no public school facilities nearby for them to use. The off-reservation boarding schools benefited the communities in which they were built and served as conduits for government funds to flow into the community, so there was local pressure to maintain the boarding schools and emphasize recruitment efforts. Also, the unpreparedness of the Native American students for public education and the prejudice they encountered in public schools served as strong deterrents for public school enrollment.

In addition, many boarding school students felt that they had received a good education that altered their lives in a positive manner and encouraged other family members to follow in their footsteps, creating a family tradition and a loyalty to a particular boarding school. Although Colonel Pratt espoused an educational policy of complete assimilation, that slowly changed in the boarding schools to incorporate some Native American arts, cultural artifacts, and even language during the 20th century as a result of Commissioner Leupp's new policy direction. Despite the fact that they were essentially institutionalized, or perhaps because of it, the Native American students bonded with each other and became each other's support system with the lack of sympathetic family available.

Although the students lacked many choices in the rigid boarding school environment, they were not clay puppets to be molded into the white man's image. Many of them were able to transform their experience into a foundation for a pan-Indian rights movement. With a common language for communication (English), the children of the various tribes were able to learn about and appreciate each other's heritage, as well as the commonality of their experience. Intertribal friendships were made, never to be forgotten, and intertribal marriages took place. In acquiring a common language and an understanding of each other's cultures, the Native American students recognized the similarities of their cultures and their experiences, and thus the forging of a nationwide pan-Indian identity began. Out of this grew a national Indian rights movement, and various Indian rights organizations were founded and peopled by boarding school graduates.

One of the ironies of the boarding school movement, established in order to assimilate the Native American children and eradicate the various Native American cultures was that it provided the necessary fertile ground for a pan-Indian movement, which subsequently placed value on the retention and continuation of the various tribal languages and cultures. Although it was a completely unintended consequence, in many instances the boarding schools created the climate and forged the connections necessary for the preservation of tribal cultures.

Safety Zone Theory

Esther ("Essie") Burnett Horne's story is one example of the safety zone theory developed by noted Native American scholar Tsianina Lomawaima. She posits that the eventual incorporation of Native American language, culture, and experience into the educational curriculum was not accidental, but was carefully analyzed by government educators in order to allow what they deemed safe, or nonthreatening to the status quo and to the existing subservient status of Native Americans in American society. Thus, during the 1920s, Native American musical pieces and arts, referred to as handicrafts, such as basketry, rug weaving, and beadwork, were incorporated into the curriculum. These representative arts were probably seen as quaint and provided no challenge to the prevailing political or Judeo-Christian religious values promulgated by the off-reservation boarding schools. In Essie's words, these arts met the expectations of the American society in a nonconfrontational manner and were a source of uniqueness and pride for the students, in addition to being a source of income. The educational policymakers at that time probably saw these native arts as a means of increasing the self-sufficiency of the students in the accepted area of manual labor.

As individual boarding schools and their curricula are examined throughout history, one sees the gradual inclusion of Native American culture, which makes sense, as good teaching practices dictate that students learn best from material that is somehow relevant to them personally. Through the years, one can see Pratt's adamant rejection of anything native become reversed. Based on Lomawaima's safety zone theory, the Native American subjects that posed no threat to the status quo, such as toys, arts and crafts, and, later, songs and dances, slowly crept into boarding school student life. It wasn't until the late 1900s, when the few remaining boarding schools survived because of their emphasis on native culture, that a more robust, native-based curriculum emphasis was found in all subject areas, including history, politics, and government.

Essie's Story

Esther Burnett Horne, a young Shoshone girl, was sent to Haskell boarding school, where she was a student from 1924 to 1929. After her father's death, her mother had a difficult time raising her large family alone, even with some help from relatives. So, Essie boarded the train to Kansas with her sister Bernice and brother Gordon, while the three youngest children remained at home in Wyoming with their mother. Essie admits that the boarding school provided her with food, clothing, education, and a stable environment that she would not have had at home. "The boarding school provided a safe environment for me. . . . You see, I had security in my home until my father died, but after that we were never sure of where our next meal would come from. We didn't always have as much to eat as we needed, and we weren't eating very healthy food. My mother was grieving. . . . She wasn't home much, and we were left to pretty much fend for ourselves" (Horne, 1998, 52).

Essie describes the military routine at Haskell as having instilled her with self-discipline, which she feels is a very "Indian" character trait. She was quite aware that the purpose of the boarding school was to erase her "Indianness," and says that her friendships with the other students and her traditional values of sharing and cooperation helped her to survive culturally. She also credits her two favorite teachers, Ella Deloria and Ruth Muskrat Bronson, both Native Americans, with introducing Native American materials into the curriculum whenever possible and instilling the students with pride in their heritage. In fact, Essie was one of the students who accompanied these teachers during her senior year to participate in community programs for churches, schools, and service organizations. The programs included music and public speaking about their Native American heritage. Essie comments that it exposed the participating students to a world outside the boarding school. "I suppose one could say that this was a 'safe' way of being Indian, that is, according to the expectations of white society. But for us it was not this way. With Ruth and Ella as our Indian mentors, these excursions became an expression of our Indianness that may not otherwise have been possible, given the poverty and discrimination so prevalent on most reservations" (Horne, 1998, 49).

Inspired by her Native American teachers, Essie returned to Haskell to attend normal school and become a boarding school teacher herself at Wahpeton, North Dakota. She married a fellow student, a Hoopla Indian from California, and even exerted her influence to have her three younger siblings accepted by Haskell, which she thought would provide a better environment than their home environment. Despite its drawbacks, Horne believes that Haskell provided her with a much safer and more wholesome environment growing up than was available within her family.

Extracurricular Programs

Like Carlisle, Haskell boasted a strong and admired sports program, as well as a military style band. The boarding school offered many extracurricular activities in order to keep the students busy and active. The children had choir, band, debate clubs, glee clubs, art classes, and the theater department to choose from. The theater group performed Henry Wadsworth Longfellow's *Hiawatha* as well as other classic plays, including those of Shakespeare. Outside lecturers and speakers were invited to present to the students, provided their messages were morally uplifting and coincided with the boarding school's educational policies. The 1919–20 school calendar shows that moving pictures were shown on the second and fourth Fridays of each month. On Saturdays the school held lawn socials, band concerts, parties, and athletic events. Every other Saturday afternoon, either the boys or the girls were able to go to town and hang out at "the shack," an off-campus store that sold refreshments and sundry items such as gum and candy bars. On Sundays, the students were required to attend Christian religious services, after choosing from a number of denominations, and met with clubs or had watermelon socials in the afternoons. The holidays were always celebrated at Haskell, much to the students' enjoyment. It was a fun and easy way to introduce the students to the prevailing American culture.

Haskell Institute, located near Lawrence, Kansas, grew to become the largest government-run Native American boarding school in the United States in 1905. Here the students are gathered on the campus in school uniforms for a photograph taken May 11, 1908. (Library of Congress)

The Haskell Indian Orchestra Band even signed a contract to travel throughout the country and perform on the Midwestern Chautauqua circuit in 1919. The boarding school students were able to travel and to present an approved, carefully orchestrated appearance of "civilized" Indians for their curious audiences. "Their performance had to be devoid of any offensive or controversial elements, 'safe' for predominantly Anglo-Chautauqua audiences to hear and see" (Vuckovic, 2008, 142–43). Nonetheless, the travel experience broadened the student musicians' horizons and debuted their roles as cultural brokers in American society. As circumscribed and sanitized as their programs were, the students reveled in sharing their native culture with the rest of America.

Haskell's sports teams, including football, basketball, and track, offered an outlet for the young men who were able to transfer their traditional physical training to the American sports arena. The indefatigable runners from the pueblos became track stars, and the winning football team traveled and played throughout the country, offering the students a broader horizon, and an acceptable outlet for competing, and winning, against Anglo-American high school teams. While the school's founders may have seen sports as one more method for assimilating the Native American students into the dominant culture, the students enthusiastically participated in the sports, turning them into a celebration of their own capabilities. The culmination of this was the 1926 Haskell homecoming celebration, at which more than 1,600 Native Americans gathered to dedicate the new athletic stadium, which was built with Haskell labor and a $250,000 donation from Native Americans, who wished to honor Haskell's national domination in the field of sports. The massive homecoming celebration featured Native American tipis, arts, and foods, as well as the pomp and ceremony of the stadium dedication itself.

Advanced Curricula

In addition to the regular grammar school curriculum offered to the students, including history, math, and English, the Haskell Institute eventually offered two advanced, two-year courses for which students were eligible after completing the eight-year grammar school course. Haskell had a normal school for training teachers, but its commercial or business school was quite well-known and unique. Classes included business arithmetic and English, bookkeeping, shorthand, typewriting, debate, law, and civics. Graduates were able to pass the U.S. Civil Service exam and find jobs as typists, stenographers, and clerks. Many were employed by the Indian Service, and some graduates found jobs in other government services. This course was known for placing all of its graduates in jobs, and so had more applicants than places for students.

Health

Despite general health improvements in the United States, Indian boarding schools continued to be unhealthy places for students. In past years, Carlisle lost many students due to the spread of tuberculosis, which continued to be a problem at Haskell into the 20th century. Horne's memoir mentions the poor nutrition of the students' diets, and the fact that it was common knowledge that the dorms contained rats. The 1928 Meriam Report, prepared by a task force set up by the Institute for Government Research and headed by Lewis Meriam, investigated health conditions at Indian boarding schools, citing inadequate funds and few trained health personnel as key reasons for poor health conditions at the schools. The two greatest communicable diseases were tuberculosis and trachoma, and the living conditions at the boarding schools exacerbated rather than prevented the spread of disease. Overcrowded conditions and shared towels were common conditions lending themselves to the rapid spread of disease. In addition, the report found that most of the schools were unable to provide an adequate diet for the students, which led to general poor health and depressed immune systems, again exacerbated by overwork with the demanding details assigned to the students, who provided almost all of the labor that kept the school running. Haskell was by no means unique in its poor care of the students; similar or worse conditions prevailed throughout the boarding school system.

An earlier health inspection at Haskell (1908) resulted in 57 students being sent home with active tuberculosis; measles and mumps epidemics were later reported at the school. During the influenza epidemic of 1918, approximately 500 of Haskell's 750 students were affected. A health inspection during 1913 revealed that some 43 percent of students had trachoma, a painful and infectious eye disease. A 1914 health report discovered that dental disease was rampant, with 2,660 cavities reported. Only a small percentage of dental problems were addressed, due to lack of funds. Although Haskell had a hospital built on campus, which allowed for the isolation and treatment of some illnesses, the sheer inadequacy of funds, personnel, and basic preventative health care overwhelmed the efforts of the available health care workers.

The Haskell Story After 1927

By 1927, Haskell's high school classes were accredited by the state of Kansas, and it began to offer post–high school courses. Part of Haskell's draw continued to be its athletic teams; its football teams were legendary through the 1930s. By 1935, Haskell's academic curriculum evolved into a post–high school vocational/technical school, and the high school classes were phased out by 1965. In 1970, under the new name of Haskell Indian Junior College, the school began offering a junior college curriculum, and in 1993 it became Haskell Indian Nations University. Today, the university's enrollment exceeds 1,000 students each semester, representing tribes from throughout the United States. It offers a wide variety of associate degrees for direct employment or for transfer to another baccalaureate program, and also offers baccalaureate degrees in environmental science, American Indian studies, elementary education, and business. Haskell is an example of a former off-reservation boarding school that transformed itself into a modern institution of higher education focused on Native American education.

References

Adams, David Wallace. *Education for Extinction: American Indians and the Boarding School Experience, 1875–1928*. Lawrence: University Press of Kansas, 1995.

Archuleta, Margaret L., Brenda J. Child, and K. Tsianina Lomawaima, eds. *Away from Home: American Indian Boarding School Experiences, 1879–2000*. Phoenix, AZ: Heard Museum, 2000.

Horne, Esther Burnett, and Sally McBeth. *Essie's Story: The Life and Legacy of a Shoshone Teacher*. Lincoln: University of Nebraska Press, 1998.

Vuckovic, Myriam. *Voices from Haskell: Indian Students Between Two Worlds, 1884–1928*. Lawrence: University Press of Kansas, 2008.

FIVE

Chilocco Indian Agricultural School (1920s–1930s)

CHILOCCO INDIAN AGRICULTURAL SCHOOL opened in 1884, five years after Carlisle opened and the same year as the Haskell Institute in Kansas. It was located on the flat plains of northern Oklahoma, in Indian Country, and because the lights shining from its original four-story building could be seen for miles at night, the institution was informally referred to as Prairie Light. Chilocco was modeled after Carlisle and featured a strictly scheduled day, vocational and academic training, and military discipline. Similar to Carlisle, students wore uniforms and slept in dormitories separated by gender and age. Government subsidies via the Indian Civilization Fund to mission-based schools were reduced in the 1880s and 1890s and eliminated entirely by the turn of the century. From that point, off-reservation boarding schools were established and funded by the U.S. government. In the early 1930s, there were 21 off-reservation boarding schools with a student population of 12,650, and 51 boarding schools on the reservations established by either the U.S. government or the tribe, with 11,590 students. Government-established off-reservation boarding schools flourished from the 1890s through the 1930s, with the enrollments peaking in the 1930s as a result of the Great Depression.

Historic Context: World War I and the Great Depression

After the conclusion of World War I in 1919, and decades after the last peace treaty was signed with the American Indians, the European American fear and hatred of the Native American population diminished. The last of the country's battles with American Indian tribes ended before the turn of the century, and open warfare had ceased. Native Americans were still not considered citizens of the United States and, as such, were ineligible for the draft. When the United States entered World War I, citizenship status was awarded to Native American men who volunteered to serve in the armed forces and completed a tour of duty. Approximately 10,000 Native American men fought in World War I, which helped change feelings about the Native American people in the United States. In 1924, all Native Americans in the United States were declared citizens with passage of the Indian Citizenship Act by Congress.

During the 1920s and 1930s, poverty among the Native American population, which was exacerbated by the Dawes Allotment Act at the turn of the century, continued and then worsened with the economic freefall during the Great Depression. Off-reservation boarding schools were often used by Native American parents as a last resort in desperate times. In struggling single-parent families and in families hit hard economically, there was the option to send their children to a boarding school, in the hope that they would not only receive an education but would be better housed, fed, and clothed than at home. While the boarding schools frequently fell short of this ideal, they did at least offer a choice to Native American families under stress.

Increasingly during the 20th century, Native American children were educated in local public schools, especially at the elementary school level. By this time, it was recognized that the most desirable form of education for all young children was local education, with the children living with their own families. In the event that the families resided in a very remote area where no public education was available, or the children experienced hostility and discrimination in the local public schools, the off-reservation boarding schools again offered another choice for the Native American parents. A large number of elementary school-age students that ended up in boarding schools during this era were orphans. David Wallace Adams notes that "by the late 1920s, nearly half of boarding school enrollments were in off-reservation schools" (Adams, 1995, 59). He concludes that a very high number of Native Americans during this time experienced a boarding school education that resulted in the boarding school becoming a part of the Native American history. Adams also stated that this signaled acceptance of the idea that removal from tribal and home influences was necessary for successful education and assimilation into American society.

Chilocco's Educational Program

By the 1920s, the rest of the American workforce was migrating from farm to factory, but the Indian schools continued to emphasize agricultural, mechanical, and construction trades in their vocational training.

K. Tsianina Lomawaima suggests that "the idea of an 'appropriate' education for Indians fit educators' preconceived notions of racial minorities' 'appropriate' place in American society, as manual laborers supporting America's agrarian economic sector" (Lomawaima, 1994, 66). During the 1920s, Chilocco's students spent half days in academic classes, and half days in vocational training for the young men or home economics classes for the young ladies. In addition, the students spent a great many hours on work details, cleaning, repairing, and maintaining the physical facilities at Chilocco. As with other Native American boarding schools, Chilocco's government allocation was too meager to actually sustain the school, so in the name of education and preparation for their future lives, students were expected to polish floors, launder clothing, repair equipment and furniture, and even build new buildings.

In 1929, the excessive drudgery of this program was recognized, and the educational program changed. The new plan assigned the students' time to 50 percent academic classes, 25 percent to art, music, and physical education classes, and 25 percent to vocational studies. However, congressional appropriations to the school did not change as the program changed, so students continued to spend a good deal of time on the work details necessary for the physical maintenance of the school. Lomawaima's interviews of Chilocco graduates show that their memories of work details are more numerous and detailed than memories of their academic history at Chilocco. In the 1930s, "Chilocco boys could pursue printing, commercial baking, butchering, construction and repair, masonry, painting, electrical wiring, shoe and harness making and repair, power plant maintenance and plumbing, or general mechanics" (Lomawaima, 1994, 68). It was probably no accident that the vocational trades taught at Chilocco were precisely the skills needed to run and maintain a large boarding school complex, and that the major employer of boarding school graduates was the government, which provided jobs in boarding schools and at Indian agencies.

But the premier program at Chilocco was its agricultural program; it continued to be the flagship agricultural school in the national boarding school system until after World War II, into the 1950s. Back in the 1930s, Chilocco was famous for raising beef cattle, dairy cattle, Morgan horses, and poultry. The students grew grain, hay, and other livestock feed and established fruit orchards and vegetable plots. The agricultural program not only provided food for the school, but sales of agricultural products supplemented the school's stingy appropriation and kept the doors open.

One unique aspect of Chilocco's agricultural program for its graduates was the homesteading program. Agriculture, never as popular as the trade

Most underfunded Native American boarding schools relied heavily on student labor to keep the schools running. Here, students at Chilocco Agricultural Indian School work in the garden, which probably supplied most of the vegetables on the table at mealtimes. (National Archives)

programs, faced the handicap of graduating students from the agricultural program who had no land upon which to establish a farm or ranch, thanks to the combined aftereffects of the treaty era and the Dawes Act. In order to entice students into the agricultural program and overcome this handicap, Chilocco made available to graduates of the agricultural program 15 homesteads on school property. If selected, the graduate could lease and farm the homestead, provided with a house and appropriate farm equipment. Popular in the 1930s, this program eventually disappeared along with the agricultural program itself during the following decade.

The Outing Program

The outing program originally established by Colonel Richard Pratt at Carlisle at the turn of the century was a popular and important program at most boarding schools up to this point. It served many purposes, not the least of which was to blatantly promote assimilation by immersing students into American households where they had to speak English and labor for European Americans. It also provided the students from broken families, or who could not afford to return home for the summers, a place to stay and a stipend.

During the 1930s, the adamant exclusion of all Native American culture from boarding school life diminished along with the general population's fear of Native Americans. The outing program began losing popularity, but whether it continued or not depended upon the individual boarding school and its circumstances. Chilocco never was able to generate a strong outing program, and it dwindled by the time the 1930s rolled around for several reasons. One of the main reasons was that many student workers were necessary to maintain Chilocco's large agricultural concerns over the summer break, so they naturally employed many of their own students. Another reason was Chilocco's location in Oklahoma. Many of the students were close enough to home that returning to their families for the summer was reasonable and desirable, since Chilocco drew the majority of its students from the local area, unlike Carlisle, which pioneered the outing system. Also, location played a darker role in the weakness of the outing system at Chilocco. The white Americans in the Oklahoma area remained unfriendly toward their Native American neighbors and had no desire to sponsor young students in their homes. Memories of conflict with the Indians were still too close for the westerners, unlike the European Americans on the eastern seaboard.

Boarding School Location

Pratt and the Christian reformers saw the off-reservation boarding school as an essential tool for assimilating Native American children into the greater American society. Pratt's original idea was to locate all such boarding schools in fully civilized communities (i.e., in the eastern United States) where, it was felt, civilization had reached its highest level and prejudice against the Native Americans was at its lowest level. However, after Carlisle opened, all the subsequent boarding schools, including both Haskell and Chilocco, were established in the western part of the United States. The chief reason for this policy change was financial; the transportation of thousands of students back and forth across the country was very expensive for a government that had difficulties from the outset in adequately funding Indian boarding schools. Also, the western states quickly grasped the fact that the establishment of a government institution in their community brought in federal funds, and an outing program provided cheap labor. In other words, an Indian boarding school could be a moneymaker in a community, so the western states began to lobby for them. Eventually, even the most ardent assimilationists had a difficult time justifying so much time spent away from home and family and viewed summers at home as a desirable combination with years spent in the boarding school. Student runaways were always a problem and concern at the boarding schools, and inherent dangers were minimized by having the boarding schools somewhat closer to home.

Desertion and Runaway Problems

One problem that all boarding schools had to cope with from the very beginning was that of runaways. Their students were children who were far away from home, many for the first time. Their introduction to boarding school was usually harsh, consisting of having their clothes and belongings taken away, their hair cut and/or deloused, and uniform clothing assigned. The children were assigned dormitory beds based on age and gender and quickly learned that mealtime was not leisurely, and the food was different and not plentiful. Days were filled with chores and activities with little to no free time, and students moved when bells were rung. It is little wonder that no matter the institution or the era, children were homesick, and homesick children left to go home, sometimes with devastating consequences.

There were runaway problems at all the boarding schools, from Carlisle on. The students, either homesick or frustrated with their institutional life or both, would simply leave school and head home despite measures taken at the boarding school to prevent this very thing. Both parents and school officials worried for the safety of the children and rightfully so. There were documented instances of students who ran away during the winter season freezing to death from exposure.

Runaways were expressing resistance to the regimented institutional life at the boarding schools in an extreme manner; other methods of resistance abounded. The schools established curfews and often had night patrols to minimize running away. Local towns were notified of runaways, and the boarding schools even offered rewards for runaways turned in by local townfolk. After all, they were dependent upon maintaining student enrollment in order to keep their allocated government funding. Among some local Native American communities near to boarding schools, harboring runaways without notifying authorities became their method of resistance.

Native American students worked diligently in their classrooms, such as this one at the Chilocco Agricultural Indian School in 1913. However, less scheduled classroom seat time and English as a second language combined to provide a poor academic foundation compared with most public schools. (National Archives)

Chilocco was no different regarding runaways. Despite the rigid routines and nightly bed checks, the students were adept at evading the authorities, and during one four-month period in 1927, Chilocco school records listed 18 girls and 111 boys as deserters. Runaways occurred most frequently at the beginning of school, when the students were the most homesick. Another spate of runaways usually occurred on Chilocco's first Town Day, when students were allowed to take their earned money to the local town to spend. Chilocco was one of the boarding schools that offered a reward to surrounding law officials and citizens for information leading to the return of a runaway—three to five dollars per student.

Lomawaima interviewed a Chilocco graduate who went on to become a schoolteacher herself. Looking back at her boarding school years, "Florence" commented that there were so many things that they *could* have done [at Chilocco], just basically a different philosophy and different approach, to have provided the kind of atmosphere that would have kept students from running away. That was a big problem, the news was always who ran away, who got caught, who was brought back, and so on. (Lomawaima, 1994, 120)

Another historian, Brenda Child, examined the history of runaways in her book *Boarding School Seasons*. She discovered that the students' reasons for running away varied. Isaac Plenty Hoops ran away from Haskell because he was tired of the boarding school diet. Charlie "deserted" Flandrau boarding school, dissatisfied with his assignment on the farm work detail, since he wished to learn a trade at school. Two other Ojibwa girls who ran away from Flandrau offered this explanation: "We wanted to go home because we were just sick of this place" (Child, 1998, 89). Many children ran away, or deserted, because of extreme loneliness and homesickness.

Parents naturally reacted with concern to the news of their child's runaway status. They feared their children would be hurt or suffer from exposure making their way home alone. Usually, students were either caught and returned to school or made it home. However, some runaways took off with a friend and ended up having an adventure. Others had horrible accidents on their journeys, and some even died.

The schools responded in various ways as well. Carlisle had an old gunpowder storage room that was used as an ad hoc jail to incarcerate returning runaways. At Chilocco, a similar guardhouse was torn down after the turn of the century, but the dormitories each had a "lockup" room, where returnees were locked in at night and suffered on a bread-and-water diet for a few days. At Haskell, runaways were usually punished by having to run through the "belt line," which consisted of two lines of students who would whip the miscreant with their belts as he or she ran past them.

Haskell had a bad year in 1910, when 53 students ran away in September, and in October there were 35 deserters and 21 in November. Some returned voluntarily after suffering from the hunger and cold and some were brought back by local police who were paid three dollars for assisting the school in this manner. In general, more boys deserted from boarding school than girls. When the girls ran away, the reason given was usually homesickness.

Given the complete institutionalization of the boarding schools, and the total lack of control that the Native American students had over all aspects of their lives at boarding school, it is not surprising that resistance took on a variety of forms, and that desertion, the ultimate resistance, was quite common. Over the years, running away persisted, and boarding schools established a variety of responses, but none was ever able to successfully deal with the runaway problem.

Life at Chilocco: Curtis Carr

Curtis Carr attended Chilocco boarding school from 1927 to 1935, and describes his student life at the boarding school to Lomawaima in the book *They Called it Prairie Light*. He went in as a younger child in an era when the government was striving to reserve the off-reservation boarding school education for older children. The young boys at Chilocco banded together in gangs for self-protection and comfort, and strong friendships were created. This boarding school was lucky to have a superintendent who was firm but fair in his dealings with the children. He also stayed in the position for a long time, so the school benefited from his consistency over the years.

One of the first things that made an impact on a child was the food and accommodations. Carr describes mealtimes, at which six to eight children sat at a table, food was placed on the table, a bell was rung, and pandemonium ensued. He advised that quickness was the trait necessary for anyone wishing to eat at all, since the food bowls were grabbed in the blink of an eye. Later, when the meal system changed and waiters served the students at table, Carr figured out that volunteering to be a waiter ensured a steady diet, since they got to eat first before serving the other students. Carr began his student career in the largest of the dormitories, which held 40 to 50 beds for young boys. There were smaller dormitories, and as students got older and more responsible, they were able to graduate to better quarters.

Like most of the Chilocco students, Carr did not work in an outing program; he stayed at the school during the summer to work for money. He recalls cutting grass all day long with a push mower for 25 cents a day during one summer vacation. His other summer jobs over the years included working for the butcher to take employee orders and fulfill them at the school's butcher shop, working on the paint crew and in the carpenter shop, building and repairing items for the school. The young boys inevitably worked at dull, repetitive tasks, but the older boys were often placed in positions of authority in the trade shops and were able to direct projects and other students. Carr was able to earn spending money, and recalled that the popular thing for boys to purchase in town was tailor-made bell-bottom trousers. The students may have been forced to wear military uniforms on campus, but were able to assert themselves and wear their own clothing during their time away from school.

Curtis rebelled against the rigid institutionalization of the boarding school by participating in a bootleg still project on the grounds. "We got fruit, peaches, and put those in a barrel one time, and water and sugar and malt or whatever, we put in that thing and let that ferment. That stuff stank to high heaven, [Laughter] you could smell it! I don't know how, why they never found any of those things, because all you had to do was get downwind of that, and you knew what was *there*" (Lomawaima, 1994, 141).

Curtis, one son of a struggling single mother who sent two sons to boarding school because of financial problems, entered Chilocco at a young age and became one of the students who ran away from the institution several times, only to be found and returned. Finally, he ran away in 1935 and never returned; never finishing high school at the boarding school. Like many other unemployed men of the time, he lived a hobo life, jumping trains and working at odd jobs. He finally settled down, put himself through high school, and joined the National Guard, which was mobilized during World War II. After the war, he worked at an aircraft company, then as an engineering photographer and business forms salesman. He married, had children, and finished his college education on the GI Bill.

Student Discipline

The students' lives at Chilocco were governed by the bugle, which sounded 22 times a day. They wore uniforms and marched close-order drills. Discipline was based on a system of demerits, which lost a student privileges and/or earned them a place on a work detail waxing the hallways or cleaning bathrooms. Serious offenses such as drunkenness or running away might result in time spent in the lockup room or, for boys, assignment to the rock pile, breaking down big rocks with a sledgehammer to go into the rock crusher. Despite the strict disciplinary system, students delighted in circumventing it. In Lomawaima's book, Chilocco alums fondly reminisce about how the girls avoided wearing the required long bloomers under their dresses to the school dances or how some of the boys would sneak out at night to a still they had hidden on the grounds for some terrible bootleg alcohol, or how they would borrow some of the school's horses for a midnight ride.

Many of those interviewed had fond memories of the boarding school, even with the regimented lifestyle and strict disciplinary system. Looking back through the years as adults some saw the discipline as a good thing that had positive results in their lives. Others conceded grudgingly that it didn't hurt. But despite the loyalty of the graduates who were interviewed, Chilocco, like other boarding schools, had plenty of students who did not thrive. The interviews showed that the experiences of the Chilocco alumni differed. Some described their boarding school experience as a positive one that contributed to their success in later life; some saw it as a more neutral experience, neither helping nor hurting their adult life; and others experienced it as a destructive period in their lives that had to be overcome in order to lead a successful, normal life. For yet others, the boarding school experience completely destroyed their lives.

Chilocco: The Final Chapter

From a 8,640-acre tract of land in northern Oklahoma with a single limestone building on it to a large complex with more than 100 buildings including a dining hall, machine shop, barns, commissary, student union, and employee cottages, Chilocco grew to be one of the largest off-reservation boarding schools in the nation. It was originally established by Major James Haworth on Chilocco Creek and opened in 1884. In 1927, Chilocco's elementary school closed due to declining enrollment, although the general enrollment at the school rose in the 1930s during the Great Depression.

A large number of Chilocco alums served in World War II, and in 1949, a large number of Navajo students came to Chilocco to be educated. Previously, Chilocco graduates were mostly from the Cherokee, Creek, and Choctaw tribes. During the 1950s, Chilocco had an enrollment of nearly 1,300 students from tribes all over the United States. The school's enrollment began to decline in the 1960s, and in 1980 the U.S. Congress ceased funding and recommended closure of the off-reservation boarding school, citing the high per-student cost of this educational option.

The outer campus lands were awarded to five local tribes: Kaw, Ponca, Otoe-Missouri, Pawnee, and Tonkawa. The main campus of 165 acres, including the school's buildings, continues to be jointly owned and is governed by the nonprofit Chilocco Benefit Association, which was established by the Council of Confederated Chilocco Tribes. The campus buildings were first leased to Narcanon, a substance abuse rehabilitation organization, from 1989 to 2001. Currently, the campus is used by the Oklahoma State University Multi-Spectral Laboratory, and plans are afoot for fund-raising in order to renovate the buildings and have the school listed as a national historical landmark. Annual reunions of former Chilocco students continue, and the Chilocco National Alumni Association has its own website to keep the memory and history of Chilocco Indian Agricultural School alive.

References

Adams, David Wallace. *Education for Extinction: American Indians and the Boarding School Experience, 1875–1928*. Lawrence: University Press of Kansas, 1995.

Child, Brenda J. *Boarding School Seasons: American Indian Families, 1900–1940*. Lincoln: University of Nebraska Press, 1998.

Lomawaima, K. Tsianina. *They Called It Prairie Light: The Story of Chilocco Indian School*. Lincoln: University of Nebraska Press, 1994.

Reyhner, Jon, and Jeanne Eder. *American Indian Education: A History*. Norman: University of Oklahoma Press, 2004.

Vuckovic, Myriam. *Voices from Haskell: Indian Students Between Two Worlds, 1884–1928*. Lawrence: University Press of Kansas, 2008.

SIX

Chemawa and Pipestone Indian Schools (1930s–1940s)

THE INDIAN BOARDING SCHOOLS run by the U.S. government during the 1930s and 1940s were most often used as child care placements of last resort. Gone were the days of aggressively recruiting Native American children for the schools, often to the point of forcing them into the schools. Most of the students during this time were in boarding school voluntarily for pragmatic reasons: desperate family financial situations (the Indian reservations suffered mightily during the Depression and were slow to recover); the death of one or both parents; parents in jail; or an abusive or inadequate home situation.

The boarding schools had finally changed from Richard Pratt's original model at Carlisle. While the mission to assimilate the Native American children into the dominant American culture was the same, it was no longer forbidden for the children to communicate in their native languages, if they knew them. By this time, the government recognized the pitfalls and inadequacies inherent in the off-reservation boarding school system, and was systematically closing the boarding schools, preferring that Native American children be educated in local schools close to their families. At this time it was the educated Native American adults who objected to the U.S. government closing the schools and reneging on their treaty promises to educate the Native American children, viewing the boarding schools as a community asset and their closure as a violation of their remaining historic treaty rights.

Historical Context: The New Deal

The Meriam Report of 1928 was the beginning of the end for many off-reservation boarding schools, including Chemawa in Oregon. Months of fieldwork resulted in a report that demonstrated that most Native Americans were living on the fringes of society in extreme poverty, which was an indication that the schools had failed abysmally in their mission to assimilate Indians into the mainstream of American society. In addition, examination of the students attending the boarding schools showed that only about 10 percent of the students were full-blood Indians; the remaining students were mixed blood and, in the minds of the government officials, could just as well be educated in their local public schools.

As a result of the Meriam Report, many off-reservation government boarding schools were closed, and there was a strong effort to mainstream the Indian students into local community day schools for their education. Reforms recommended for the remaining boarding schools included the inclusion of native culture into the curriculum, higher standards of care for the children, inclusion of high school grades, increased qualifications for teachers, improved academic and vocational curricula, and a decrease in the use of student labor. These reforms were supposed to occur in the midst of the Great Depression, so the changes came slowly, because they were unfunded, but change did occur.

In 1933, John Collier was appointed commissioner of Indian affairs, and he worked with education directors Will Carson Ryan Jr. and William Beatty to change Indian education policy. Chemawa was temporarily closed in the spring of 1933, but public outcry from senators, local citizens, and Native Americans caused the Oregon school to reopen in the fall. In 1934, the Indian Reorganization Act ended the carving up of reservation land into individual allotments (Dawes Act) and promoted local control of schools, Indian self-government, student loans for Indians, and the addition of native-based curricula. Also known as the Indian New Deal, this increased the pressure to close off-reservation boarding schools and forced further improvements and reforms within the boarding school community.

Chemawa's Educational Program

In 1935, Chemawa's program was changed so that during the first year, boys rotated through sheet metal, plumbing, carpentry, painting, farming, metal work, leather repair, and auto shop; in subsequent years they specialized in one of the offerings. While the girls continued to be trained in domestic education, the addition of practice houses gave each young woman a chance to manage a budget and the entire operation of a home instead of merely participating in chore work.

A Bureau of Indian Affairs study in 1939 showed that there was little correlation between the vocational courses taken by the boys at Chemawa and their subsequent employment back on their reservations. It was critical of the continued emphasis by the school on vocational training over academic instruction. As a result, in 1940 a reservation survey course was initiated, in which the Native American students were divided into homerooms by tribal affiliation, where they learned about their own reservations, studied tribal council minutes, and debated the current issues on their own reservations. "It was hoped that students would become familiar with their reservation environment, eventually taking their place in the reservation community. Instruction on the Indian Reorganization Act included allotment, purchase of lands, educational loans, organization of tribes, self-government, citizenship and management and supervision of tribal resources" (Bonnell, 1997, 76). Lawney Reyes recalls extensive vocational training options at Chemawa during the 1940s, when students could train for the following jobs: auto mechanic, barber/beautician, blacksmith, business owner, carpenter, chef, dairy worker, electrician, farmer, gardener, home nurse, janitor, laundry/dry cleaner, leather worker, machinist, painter, plumber, printer, sheet-metal worker, shoemaker, tailor/seamstress, waitperson, and welder (Reyes, 2002, 118). The typical school day still consisted of a half day of academics and a half day of vocational training for blue-collar employment.

New Deal Boarding School Days

Adam Fortunate Eagle, born Adam Nordwall, attended Pipestone Indian Boarding School in Minnesota from 1935 to 1945. His memoir concentrates on recollections of his time at the school, focusing on relationships, vocational training and extracurricular activities rather than the academics of the boarding school. Like so many other students, Adam and his brothers and sisters attended the boarding school after their father's death because of the dire financial circumstances in which their mother was left and the poverty in which they lived.

Like every other child entering the boarding school, Adam's first experience was a shower down in the basement, where his old raggedy clothing was discarded. A lice comb was run through his hair, and at the first sign of lice, he was sent to get a haircut and have a salve rubbed all over his head. Naked, he was examined, and another salve was put on a rash in his crotch. However, his account of his experiences does not reflect the fear and hatred in many earlier boarding school accounts; it is balanced by the fact that he was safe and warm in a dormitory with other friends, looked after by a caring house mother. He had the benefit of hot and cold running water with daily showers and learned how to use a flush toilet. He was well fed and supplied with better clothing than he has previously owned.

During the Indian New Deal, children were not discouraged from speaking their native languages, although by this time, fewer were familiar with their native languages than in previous years. As Adam Fortunate Eagle notes, the children were punished for cursing, not for speaking their native languages. Likewise, there was no effort to belittle or suppress Native American culture in the new boarding schools. In fact, by this time, many of the teachers and employees of the boarding schools were Native Americans. However, the boarding schools were still complete institutions, with all of the issues of controlling large numbers of children in their daily lives. The institution was still run on a strict schedule and the children still moved through their days with bells signaling their next move, even though they no longer marched through the hallways in military formation.

The boarding school menus improved through the years, and a typical Thursday menu at Pipestone looked like this:

Breakfast: Cracked wheat with raisins, brown bread, cereal, butter, whole milk, coffee
   Dinner: Roast beef, brown gravy, steamed potatoes, stewed tomatoes, bread, cornbread, fruit Betty, whole milk
   Supper: Scalloped corn, dill pickles, bread, peanut butter, stewed apricots, cake, hot tea, whole milk. (Fortunate Eagle, 2010, 39)

The students all had to work hard to keep the school running; Pipestone had a farm, dairy, bakery, and carpentry shop. They had a traditional program of working half days and academic schooling half days, but they had fun, too. In addition to school dances and socials, the boys had a special place where they parched corn after working the corn harvest. The boys also enjoyed going hunting in their spare time, attending movies and newsreels in the movie house of the nearby town, and visiting the local quarry for which the boarding school was named. Adam's lifelong visits led him to become a pipestone calumet artist and to lobby for the preservation of the sacred quarry. Students went home for summer if they had adult supervision and attended local Fourth of July powwows if they spent their summers at Pipestone.

During this time period, there were many extracurricular activities available for students living at boarding schools. In 1940, Chemawa students could join the literary clubs, student council, orchestra, band, Letterman's Club, Indian Club, Boys Glee Club, Girls Glee Club, choir, YMCA, and other religious-based organizations. Many of the boarding school teachers and staff at Chemawa were Native Americans, and the students generally enjoyed good relationships with them. A 14-year-old Chemawa student attending around 1940 spoke about the annual pageant at Chemawa: "Then we had what we called an annual pageant. It was kinda an annual celebration of the Chemawa birthday. . . . I know a couple years we practiced and practiced. . . . We all made our [dresses], they were made out of white muslin, but you fringed 'em and from a distance it looked like buckskin. We all did, I think the [*sic*] from the Southwest, the Corn Dance. Oh, I thought that was the most beautiful thing I ever saw. That we were part of something. That was always an honor, we were all proud. Then they had the white people all [come and they] sat in the bleachers, oohed and aahed" (Bonnell, 1997, 80–81). Lawney Reyes, who attended Chemawa in 1940–1942, wrote in his memoir, "I did not experience any harsh restraint against Indian culture or tradition at Chemawa. Generations of Indians before me had

Most of the Native American boarding schools had popular and successful athletic programs. Pictured is the Chemawa Indian School (Salem, Oregon) baseball team, in 1939. (National Archives)

already felt the full force of that practice. I learned that in earlier years, speaking the Indian language had been forbidden. During my time, efforts to teach the white way were still in force, but attempts to abolish or restrain Indian culture were past. The practice of Indian culture, however, was not encouraged or discussed" (Reyes, 2002, 117).

The Outing Program

The outing program, once thought to be an integral part of the off-reservation boarding school program, is no longer a significant element of the Indian boarding school curriculum. During the 1930s and 1940s, the existence of the program was entirely dependent upon the individual boarding school situations, as decided by the superintendents. Neither Chemawa nor Pipestone had an outing program for their students. Adam Fortunate Eagle, a Pipestone student from 1935 to 1945, recalls that at a certain point, as an older student, he was advised to go into town and get an after-school job to make some spending money, but that was as close as it got. Students were able to work at summer jobs on campus, if they were unable to return home for the summer because of a lack of adult supervision at home. However, it was thought that if the family was willing and could afford the transportation, that it was desirable for the students to spend summers at home.

Boarding School Vignettes

Chemawa Indian School is located near Salem, Oregon, in the beautiful Willamette Valley. Opened in 1880, it is now the oldest continuously operating boarding school in the United States, currently teaching grades 9–12 and often referred to as Chemawa High School. Originally serving local Native American tribes from the state of Washington, Chemawa diversified in the 1940s to include a special program for Navajo Indians. The school sought to serve the entire northwest native population and also drew many Alaska Natives. Its location made Chemawa a natural choice for Alaska Natives looking for a boarding school experience.

Pipestone Indian School, located in southwestern Minnesota, opened in 1893 with one building made of locally quarried Sioux quartzite and six transfers from a Wisconsin boarding school. It grew to more than 55 buildings and included a farm, dairy farm, and employee cottages. The students received both academic and vocational training and also maintained the boarding school operation with their assigned chores. Unlike many other Indian boarding schools, it was located on the Pipestone Indian

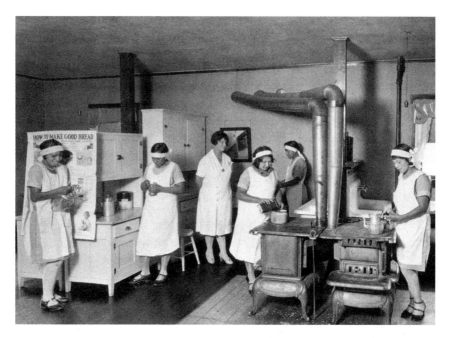

In Native American boarding schools, the male students experienced a half day of vocational training in the trades, while the female students were trained in the so-called domestic arts. Here the students at Pipestone Indian Training School (Minnesota) learn cooking skills in a 1920 home economics class. (Minnesota Historical Society)

Reservation; it was not an off-reservation boarding school, although it was supported by the government and had many students that traveled there from other reservations. It was near a town, where the students were allowed to go on a weekly basis, and also had a lot of nearby open land, where the boys hunted and played. The school was also near Pipestone National Monument, where the students often visited and learned about the importance of this sacred site and the local native heritage. Pipestone Indian School was closed in 1953.

World War II

World War II affected the entire country, and it led to lasting change for Native American education as well. Like the rest of the country, Indian boarding school students went to movie theaters in nearby towns, spending their earned money watching newsreels of Nazis. The students saw teachers enlist in the army, and indeed, the U.S. Army became the employer of choice for a generation of boys in boarding school. Of the five Nordwall brothers at Pipestone, four served in World War II, along with many of their classmates.

Fortunate Eagle details how the war affected Pipestone boarding school in his memoir. The students planted a larger "victory garden" than any installed before and scrounged scrap metal for the war effort. Pipestone staffers began to enlist, and parents and families moved to large cities to work in defense-related industries. Adam describes one school field trip where the young boys were given gunny sacks and taken out to a local lake to harvest the ripe milkweed pods before they split open, so that the fluffy insides could be packed off to be used as stuffing for life vests.

Even the boys' woodshop class got involved in the national war effort. Instructions and blueprints were sent by the government for wooden scale models of all the airplanes used in the war by the United States, England, Germany, and Japan. The boys built, painted, and decorated the wood airplane models carefully with decals according to detailed specifications, because the models would be used in U.S. flight schools to train the recruits to recognize enemy (and friendly) aircraft. Those airplanes that did not pass inspection were kept at Pipestone, and hung from the rafters. Within a short time, a tiny air force of rejects graced the Pipestone woodshop.

All of the boys were eager to become involved in World War II as warriors, and a group of boys ran away from Pipestone to enlist, only to be detained by the police after being turned in by citizens who reported seeing Japanese spies in their town. Like most of the Pipestone graduates, the boys had only completed ninth grade, and were 14 years old. They were told to come back when they were older. Most of the Pipestone graduates, including Adam Fortunate Eagle, went on to complete their education at Haskell Indian School for their high school years.

Lawney Reyes was at Chemawa at the beginning of World War II, and it impacted him as well. He remembers the excitement of all the boys at Chemawa when they learned the country was at war. They eagerly participated in pulling down all shades at night and in standing watch for a two-hour shift during the night. Lawney was personally mistaken for a Japanese person at an amusement park in Washington and attacked by some boys. Luckily, the misunderstanding was quickly cleared up.

Life at Chemawa: Lawney Reyes

Lawney Reyes and his younger sister, Luana, Lakes Indians from the Colville reservation in Washington, were sent to Chemawa in 1940, when their parents divorced and there was no one to care for them. Lawney, like many entering boarding school before him, remembers clearly his first days at Chemawa. Although he was hungry, he was taken to a place where 10 older girls waited with a vinegar and water mixture to wash his hair and rid it of lice. He found it embarrassing to be handled this way by strangers; next he was taken to the showers, which was a new experience that he liked. Then he was taken to another building, given a short haircut, and issued clothing—denim pants, shirt and jacket, underwear, socks, and black high-top shoes. He was surprised and impressed by the large number of Indian students from different tribes, but he noticed that the students from the same tribes stuck together and spoke their own language; everyone suspicious of the others.

"As days turned into weeks, tribal barriers began to break down, and we began to communicate. We were curious about the places everyone had left behind and made efforts to get to know one another. We came to understand that we all had something in common, regardless of our tribal backgrounds. Friendships formed. It was as if a new tribe was developing" (Reyes, 2002, 98).

Dorm life consisted of being awakened by a bell at 5:00 A.M. Students dressed, made their beds, and marched to the mess hall at 6:00 A.M. for breakfast, then returned to the dormitory to brush their teeth and put on clean clothing and shoes. School began at 9:00 A.M.; at noon the students ate lunch in the mess hall, and returned to classes at 1:00 P.M. Classes ended at 4:00 P.M., with supper in the mess hall at 6:00 P.M. Students were allowed free time until 8:30 P.M.; lights had to be out in the dormitory by 8:45 P.M. The boys cleaned their dormitory each Saturday and showered each Sunday night. While Lawney began by marching to and from his classes, the older boys didn't have to march; they walked everywhere. Lawney described the staff as primarily white, but his dorm matron was cold and uncaring, and her assistant was abusive. The teachers, also mostly white, were kind enough to the students but did not establish personal relationships with them.

Lawney's memoir relates how a group of boys, anxious to have some coffee, pooled their change and walked to town to purchase a communal bag of coffee. Then they found a wooded area near the school where they could make a fire, fill a can with water and, when it boiled, poured in some coffee. The boys continued this tradition on Saturday afternoons and shared stories of their lives and their people. Later, they shared songs and drummed on tree branches or makeshift drums, and those who knew them demonstrated dances from their culture. The boys even made bows and arrows and held mock battles. Lawney concludes: "These experiences helped me develop for the first time the feeling of being an Indian. Back home, I did not think of myself or our people as Indian" (Reyes, 2002, 112). He went on to say that in the struggle for survival, his people adopted the white man's ways, so he never knew his own culture. His experiences at Chemawa gave him more than a high school diploma; it was there that he learned how to be an Indian.

Lawney says that he was taught reading, writing, and arithmetic, as well as geography and history. "I noticed that the great Indian leaders like Crazy Horse, Chief Joseph, and Geronimo were not mentioned. All the heroes were white people like George Washington, Abraham Lincoln, and Thomas Jefferson" (Reyes, 2002, 120–21). Reyes goes on to say that he thought that the teachers at Chemawa were good; they just didn't know their Indian subject matter very well. "We younger boys conducted our own history courses at our coffee breaks, covering the greatness of Indian leaders, Indian warriors, and Indian ways" (Reyes, 2002, 121). The boarding school at Chemawa also introduced Reyes to art, which was to have a lasting impact, as he became an artist. Reyes speaks about the mission of the boarding schools to "civilize" the Indians. He concludes that he may have been "civilized," but that Chemawa did not separate him from his culture; it introduced him to his culture in the form of the extracurricular social activities with his fellow students.

Life at Pipestone: Adam Fortunate Eagle

Adam Fortunate Eagle, born Adam Nordwall, attended Pipestone Indian boarding school from the time he was five years old, along with his four brothers and two sisters. The youngest of the family, Adam began his life at school separated from his siblings in a dormitory with the youngest students, called the "Stink Dormitory" due to the number of bed wetters it housed. Like many other boarding school students from this era, his family's decision to send the children to boarding school was pragmatic, occurring after the death of his father, with his mother unable to care for seven children. Unlike earlier years, there was no coercion involved on the part of the government to recruit and keep students in boarding schools.

Although fully recognizing the negative aspects of full institutionalization in a boarding school, Fortunate Eagle recalls his 10 years at Pipestone with fondness and details the successful careers of siblings and friends from Pipestone to prove that the boarding school provided a good beginning and a solid foundation for its graduates. Despite the regimented days, the students were able to spend some free time together. "Most of the older Chippewa boys from Minnesota and Wisconsin know how to hunt, fish, and trap. Between the rock dam and Indian lakes is a stretch of brush and tall grass almost a half-mile long that's crisscrossed with rabbit trails. It's a good place to set snares, and we catch lots of rabbits. At the parching place we make hobo stew, out of cut up rabbit meat, potatoes, carrots, and onions, in one-gallon tin cans that sit right on the hot coals. . . . Some of the older boys really know how to cook over an open fire and show us younger guys how to do things like that" (Fortunate Eagle, 2010, 86). Fortunate Eagle also tells how the school employees are aware of the boys' "parching place," where they take some of the school's corn harvest and parch it traditionally to share with others, but consider it sacred, and leave the boys alone there.

These types of interactions served to form lifetime bonds of friendship and brotherhood between students from different tribes, and the students also learned from each other what it meant to be an Indian. Fortunate Eagle also lists the significant number of Native American school employees and discusses their positive impact on the students' lives. Clearly, for some students, the other boarding school students and staff comprised another family. Strong bonds of friendship were formed as they helped and supported each other through the institution. It is no wonder that the boarding schools were the initial birthplace of the pan-Indian movement in the United States. The bonds formed at boarding school reached across tribal boundaries, and during their free play times, the students shared their tribal knowledge, beliefs, and stories with each other. Many of the students went on to assume leadership positions in their tribes, and the network of friends formed at boarding school helped them immeasurably.

Student Discipline and Runaways

Although many of the harsh rules and restraints of earlier years no longer existed at the boarding schools, they were still total institutions housing children away from home and family for long periods. The problems of runaway children persisted throughout the history of boarding schools. Parents and school staff were not quite so fearful that unwise runaways could get lost and die from exposure while walking home, but dangers still persisted for unsupervised students fleeing the school.

In his memoir, Fortunate Eagle recalls that Joe and Cry Baby, who were homesick and lonesome, decided to run away in the dead of winter. They hopped a slow-moving freight train and were climbing off a car to hop onto another northern-moving train when Joe's hands slipped on the icy ladder, he fell, and his arm was crushed by the train. Cry Baby ran for help, and he and Joe are returned to Pipestone, where Joe's arm was amputated below the elbow in the boarding school hospital. Adam also remembers the boys from his dorm being called out to ride in the school's pickup one afternoon to hunt some runaway girls from Pipestone. The boys tracked them to a local cornfield where they tackled and captured them and brought them back to Pipestone. Fortunate Eagle never ran away from Pipestone, but he ran away from his mother's home in Oregon, when she told him she couldn't afford to send him back to Pipestone at the end of one summer. He went back to Pipestone, using the money he earned to ride the bus.

Although Pipestone's formal disciplinary policy is not addressed by Fortunate Eagle, it is clear from his stories that the mischievous boys suffered consequences for their pranks. When they booby-trapped their dorm rooms in their constant war with the boys in the other dorms, occasionally the teachers ended up getting caught in the traps. The teachers would bring out a leather strap, and everyone would have to bend over for their swat. Adam remembers being told that one small room was where they put the runaways for punishment, but he never saw anyone confined in the room.

Chemawa used a system of demerits as its primary disciplinary tool; the demerits had to be worked off by doing such chores as disinfecting restrooms and cleaning dormitory rooms. The students also suffered a loss of privileges, such as no pass to go into town, no movies, and so on. Older students were used to police the younger students, and also made up the peer court that tried and sentenced the miscreants to swats with a wooden paddle. Chemawa also had a small room for the confinement of runaways, which the students knew about, but no one ever saw it used. Reyes remarked that no one he knew ever ran away from Chemawa, since most of them didn't know how to get home from there.

One Chemawa student, Harriet, relates how she was actually sent to the school as a punishment by her white foster parents. After her parents' death, she was miserable and defiant in the foster care system, and one day her foster mother told her to pack, she was going to reform school. "So they loaded me in the car and we left. Drove, went a long ways and finally I looked. It was turning into Chemawa. Oh I was so glad, so glad. . . . I always said I thought I died and went to Indian heaven [laughter]. To see all the Indian kids all in the dining room together, or all in the auditorium, all in the bleachers at the game" (Bonnell, 1997, 78).

Chemawa and Pipestone: The Final Chapter

During the post–World War II years at Chemawa, student interviews reveal a great deal of satisfaction with the boarding school. The pressure to "de-Indianize" the students diminished in the 1950s, and the school offered students a wide range of courses in both academic and vocational fields in a setting where students often experienced far less prejudice than in local public schools. During the 1960s, the special programs for Alaska Natives and Navajos were phased out, and more local Native American students were placed at Chemawa, provided there were no other acceptable educational choices for them, such as for students living in remote rural areas and those with untenable home situations. Chemawa stepped up vocational training and job placement in urban areas as local public schools became the schools of first resort for Native American children.

There were many changes at Chemawa during the 1970s and 1980s as a result of the civil rights movement of the 1960s and the Kennedy Report issued in 1969. The tribes had increasing control over educational institutions for Native American students. During the 1970s, it was determined that a now-dilapidated Chemawa needed to either be closed or rebuilt. Local Native Americans rallied once again to save Chemawa, and the campus was given the funding to build a new alternative campus for schooling some 42 northwestern tribal areas in 1977. With the new school came problems as well as opportunities. A Bureau of Indian Affairs alcohol program operated on campus, but the school was plagued with drug and alcohol problems as well as intertribal conflict. In an era of permissiveness, there were no punishments and no consequences for totally uncontrolled behavior, and Chemawa soon gained a poor academic reputation as a "party school." The school is still open today as the Chemawa Indian School, celebrating its 130th birthday in 2010, where it continues as an educational institution for Native Americans and emphasizes Native American cultural education.

Currently, Chemawa Indian School is listed as a public high school for grades 9–12 in the Salem, Oregon, area. It is like any other accredited high school, except that due to its long history, it numbers its alumni in the thousands.

Pipestone suffered a different fate after World War II. With the change in educational policy during the 1950s, the children were sent to local public schools, and Pipestone slowly phased out their academic grades 6–9 during the early 1950s. The campus was abandoned and vacant as of 1955. Eventually, the city of Pipestone purchased the campus from the federal

Indian monument area except for 117 acres, which was reserved for the fish and game department. Subsequently, the Good Samaritan Society bid on and purchased the hospital and associated buildings for a home for the elderly, and the city sold the other campus buildings to a vocational school for a nominal fee. Unlike Chemawa, Pipestone boarding school is an institution of the past, alive only in memoirs today.

References

Bonnell, Sonciray. *Chemawa Indian Boarding School: The First One Hundred Years, 1880–1980*. Dissertation. Dartmouth College, 1997.

Fortunate Eagle, Adam. *Pipestone: My Life in an Indian Boarding School*. Norman: University of Oklahoma Press, 2010.

Reyes, Lawney L. *White Grizzly Bear's Legacy: Learning to be Indian*. Seattle: University of Washington Press, 2002.

SEVEN

Phoenix Indian School (1950s–1960s)

History and Background

THE PHOENIX INDIAN Industrial School was started in 1891, based on the
Carlisle model of education and assimilation, using a two-pronged curricula of academic classes and vocational training. Like Carlisle, the Phoenix School was originally supposed to occupy the soon-to-be-abandoned
army complex at Fort McDowell, but the Nebraska educators beginning
the school had no liking for the isolation of the run-down fort or for sharing
space with local critters such as snakes and scorpions. They opted instead
for an urban boarding school north of the small city of Phoenix, Arizona.
They were encouraged in this choice by the local businessmen, who immediately realized the financial benefits of having such a school in their town.
They were also eager to take advantage of the cheap student labor to work
in nearby cotton fields and fruit orchards. At that time, Phoenix was a city
that was quite unfriendly to Native Americans because of its proximity to
several tribal reservations and the fairly recent cessation of hostilities with
local tribes. The school was sold to the local populace on the basis that it
cost less money to educate an Indian than it did to exterminate him.

Due to the aggressive recruiting techniques of the superintendent, by
1896 the school had 12 buildings, an operating farm, and 396 students. During the first decade, none of the students achieved an eighth grade level,
and it was thought that they were less intelligent than Anglo-Americans
and would have to make a living doing menial work. The boys were enrolled in vocational programs such as carpentry, blacksmithing, tailoring,
shoemaking, harness making, and farming, although government inspec-
tors recommended that the tailoring and shoemaking programs be eliminated due to lack of usefulness. The girls learned housekeeping, sewing,
kitchen work, and laundry work. The Phoenix Indian School operated on a

traditional half day academic and half day vocational curriculum, and enthusiastically embraced the outing system, which was very popular.

As with many of the other off-reservation Indian boarding schools, the Phoenix Indian School responded to changing trends in the 1930s, when military-style uniforms were phased out and discipline became more relaxed. In response to the construction of more elementary day schools on the Arizona reservations, Phoenix Indian School focused on a high school curriculum, and the school's band and sports teams became prominent extracurricular activities. As a result of John Collier's influence, a group of linguists, artists, and teachers at the school collaborated to produce the "Little Herder" readers, which taught the written Navajo language.

Also, American Indian arts programs in general were encouraged by Collier. Lloyd Henry New, a recent Cherokee graduate from the Chicago Art Institute, joined the Phoenix Indian School as an art instructor. Students were encouraged to produce and sell their arts and crafts. Collier regarded native art as having intrinsic value as an expression of culture, and he also saw it as an occupation, a way for Native American students to make money. Several of the Phoenix Indian School's students went on to become famous artists, including Charles Loloma, the Hopi silversmith.

The Phoenix Indian School established Company F of the Arizona National Guard at the school in 1915, and its members fought bravely in World War I. In 1924, the all-Indian unit drew its participants from the students and graduates of the Phoenix Indian School, and garnered awards in the 1920s and 1930s. In 1940 the Arizona National Guard company was reactivated and expanded, becoming the renowned Bushmasters, Arizona's 158th Regimental Combat team, who served with honor in the Pacific Theater during World War II. Other Phoenix Indian School graduates served in the war as Navajo code talkers and in all other areas of service. After the end of World War II, there were suggestions that the Phoenix Indian School be closed. But a group of Navajo ex-servicemen visited Washington, DC, in 1946 and demanded that the treaty rights providing Navajo children with an education be met, and a special program for the Navajo was established at Phoenix and other Indian schools, which helped to reinvigorate the Phoenix School.

During the 1950s, the Bureau of Indian Affairs (BIA) set up a program to relocate skilled Indians from the reservations into the cities, and many returned servicemen were included in this program. The Special Navajo Program at the Phoenix Indian School was designed to prepare students for this program, and in 1958 there were 427 Navajo students in the program.

In addition to academic and vocational training, the boarding schools offered art and music classes. Pictured is an art class at Phoenix Indian School (Arizona) at the turn of the century. (National Archives)

The 1950s heralded a complete renovation of the school; the original buildings from the 1890s were demolished and a modern campus was built, featuring eight new dormitories with air conditioning and basement recreational facilities, including televisions and pool tables. There was a new administration building, library/materials center, science classrooms with labs, nine vocational and home economics units, and a warehouse. The renovation was completed in 1963 and a dedication celebration was held with a band concert, fashion show, barbeque, and Indian dances. Four of the original buildings, which were of historical interest, remained on campus.

Before the renovation, faculty were also housed on campus, which provided more interaction between faculty and students and more of a familial relationship. After the renovation, all faculty lived off-campus, and there was less involvement between teachers and students and less oversight of students. Feeding the 1,500 students and staff for the institution in the face of current changes; it was no longer self-sufficient in

The Phoenix Indian School dining hall, built in 1902, is the oldest campus building still standing after the school's closure in 1990. There are plans to renovate this historic building to house a Native American cultural center. (Library of Congress)

providing food. In 1952, the school was forced to auction off its dairy herd, because the Phoenix city boundaries had grown to encompass the school and livestock was not allowed in the city. The school leased lands from the local Pima Indians for their hog farm and from the Colorado River Indians for their cattle herd and continued to supply itself most of the meat needed by the school. A vegetable garden was still kept on the school grounds, scaled back from their World War II victory garden.

During the 1950s, the school held an annual open house when parents and friends arrived at the school to visit the campus and celebrate. The students hosted their guests for a day of campus tours and entertained them with traditional dances and a band concert, finishing with dinner for everyone. Some years, more than 1,000 attended the annual event. The school's band, begun in the best Carlisle tradition, was popular throughout the entire Phoenix community and was a big draw at parades and community celebrations in the parks. In both 1959 and 1963, the band was invited to march in the prestigious Rose Bowl Parade in Pasadena, California.

During the 1950s and 1960s, Phoenix Indian High School's sports teams established a winning tradition and filled the school's trophy case. The basketball teams were especially good, and the school also produced good football and baseball players, as well as boxers. The school newspaper, *The Redskin*, devoted a lot of ink to sports in its publications. The newspaper was printed in the campus print shop, which also did other printing jobs. Because the Special Navajo Program was also on campus, it was natural for the educators responsible for creating a written form of the Navajo language to have their Navajo readers, Bibles, and other Navajo-language materials printed at Phoenix Indian High School. The school even printed the ballots used for elections on the Navajo reservation. This special program was a precursor to later bilingual programs. Many future leaders were educated at the Phoenix Indian High School during this time, including Peterson Zah and Ivan Sidney, who both went on to college and became tribal chairmen of the Navajo and Hopi tribes, respectively.

More and more during the 1950s and 1960s, Phoenix Indian High School became similar to other public high schools in the area. In 1956 it was admitted to the Arizona Interscholastic Association to begin sports competitions with other local public high schools, instead of playing other BIA and private schools. It was accredited by the North Central Association of Colleges and Secondary Schools in 1960, and the academic program was improved to the point that the school hosted an honor society, and was the only BIA school to do so. With the new emphasis on academics and leadership, the vocational programs experienced a steady decline, and the purpose of the school was questioned. Was it time to close down the Phoenix Indian High School?

The Outing Program at Phoenix

From its inception, the outing program at the Phoenix Indian School was very popular. Hundreds of students were involved, and it became a tradition for Phoenix housewives to have an Indian domestic. Boys were hired to pick crops and do other manual labor, but the demand for girls could never be met by the boarding school. Although superficially patterned after Carlisle's outing program, the Phoenix program was quite different, according to historian Robert Trennert. "Government bureaucrats expected the outings to operate much like Carlisle's celebrated system, with Indian students living with white families on the basis of some equality, learning a middle-class occupation, and developing a desire to assimilate. But at Phoenix, as with other western schools, the outing students were treated as employees and assigned menial tasks." (Trennert, 1988, 53) Trennert also said that the Indian employees were paid less than white employees and were not expected to advance in their jobs. As early as 1900, an Indian Service inspector criticized the program as serving merely as an employment bureau for cheap menial labor.

This seemed typical of the outing programs at the western boarding schools. In the West, anti-Indian attitudes persisted strongly, and the outing program became nothing more than a way to provide cheap menial labor under the pretense of providing an educational program. The educators involved believed that the Indians were inferior human beings who were destined to either work in menial jobs or return to the reservation.

At Phoenix Indian School, the outing program became tinged with scandal, because the students were not well-supervised on their off-campus forays into the world of work. Many of the reservation Indians working in town, who were about the same age as the students, hung out around the "outing girls" and encouraged them to carouse and engage in immoral conduct. The townsfolk also had a hard time distinguishing between delinquent Indian girls from the reservation who were in town and the students. The program was shut down for awhile, but such was its popularity, it was reconstituted, with a matron to oversee the conduct of the girls. Unfortunately, a concern for the safety of the "outing girls" was not a voiced concern.

By the 1920s, the outing system was merely a name for a flourishing employment business in Phoenix, where it had become quite fashionable to employ Indian domestic servants. The outing matron was responsible for employing more than 400 Indian students and graduates in the Phoenix area. Many of the so-called students rarely or never attended any academic classes at the school. By this time, Richard Pratt's outing system was no longer recognizable. As in other boarding schools, the outing system officially ended in the 1930s at Phoenix Indian School after the critical Meriam Report was issued.

However, the outing program continued at the Phoenix Indian High School in another form well into the 1950s and 1960s. The students continued to participate in a voluntary Saturday work program off-campus, but slept in the Phoenix Indian High School dormitories. The greatest demand from the local community continued to be for female students to do housework, and there were never enough students to fill the available jobs. Local businesses also continued to hire students. Once many of the students were earning their own money, a local bank established a branch on campus, and workshops were given to the students to explain banking and money. A student store was also opened, which sold small sundries, stationery supplies, candy, and gum. Many students enjoyed both spending their earned money on campus and saving their money for summer trips home and family gifts.

Discipline and Runaways at Phoenix

The discipline of the Native American students at government-run, off-reservation boarding schools has been controversial throughout history, in part because of the great cultural differences between the Native Americans and the European Americans regarding child discipline in general. The European Americans believed that to spare the rod was to spoil the child, and corporal punishment was one commonly accepted method of discipline in American child-rearing practice, which was transplanted into the government's Indian boarding schools. The educators did not know, and many did not care, that corporal punishment was never used to discipline Native American children in their various native cultures. Corporal punishment and confinement were common punishments for runaways, although not particularly effective. Also, there were instances where shame and ridicule were used to punish students. Earlier in the school's history, one runaway girl was punished by cutting off her hair to shame and embarrass her (Trennert, 1989, 598).

More commonly used forms of discipline included a demerit system in which students who were assigned demerits for disobedience were required to work them off by doing menial chores. Also, students' privileges were revoked as a result of breaking rules.

The history of discipline at the Phoenix Indian School is reflective of that at other boarding schools, but at Phoenix it ultimately resulted in a major political controversy. Phoenix Indian School was located close to the various tribes that it served, and from the beginning, it had a runaway problem. If a student was unhappy, it was a relatively common and safe option to simply leave the school and return home. In Arizona, there was a minimal danger that runaway students might succumb to dangerously freezing weather. Usually, older male students who were known to be responsible were sent after the runaways to find them and bring them back to school. The threat of corporal punishment was used freely, but the actual instances remained few until Superintendent John Brown took over in 1917.

Helen Sekaquaptewa, who attended Phoenix Indian School during Superintendent Brown's tenure, remembered that "corporal punishment was given as a matter of course; whipping with a harness strap was administered in an upstairs room to the most unruly" (Sekaquaptewa, 1969, 136–37). She goes on to say that punishment for a girl runaway might involve cutting the grass with a scissors, wearing a card with the words "I ran away." Boys were confined in the "jail," and repeat runaway boys often had their heads shaved and were given dresses to wear (Sekaquaptewa, 1969, 137). Helen herself never experienced these punishments. The daughter of a Hostile (a Hopi Indian who opposed the mandatory education of his children in American schools), Helen defied her family in order to further her education at Phoenix Indian School, and was selected by Superintendent Brown's wife to work in their household. She remained friendly with the Brown family her entire life.

Rumors about Superintendent Brown's harsh punishments were transmitted to Indian Commissioner Charles H. Burke. No proof was uncovered for allegations against the superintendent; these issues were often difficult to investigate, particularly since the disciplinarians at the various Indian schools were often Native Americans themselves, as was the case at Phoenix. These allegations of brutality reached the ears of New York social worker and reformer John Collier, who called for a change in the policy of forced assimilation, and worked to expose the corruption in the Bureau of Indian Affairs. During the mid-1920s, the Department of the Interior authorized an investigation of Indian affairs which resulted in the 1928 Meriam Report, which was highly critical of the government's handling of Indian affairs in several arenas, including education for assimilation as practiced in the governmental boarding schools.

In 1929, Commissioner Burke issued orders that all Indian schools dismantle their jail facilities and cease confining their pupils. Further, all corporal punishment was forbidden that same year. In this, the Indian boarding schools were in advance of the rest of American public schools, which, with the exception of one state, all allowed corporal punishment until 1972. However, the corporal punishment issue at Phoenix Indian School was not laid to rest, as one employee, Mrs. Schmidt, contacted the new Indian Commissioner Charles Rhoads with continued complaints about the use of corporal punishment at Phoenix Indian School. An investigator arrived at the school and conducted more than 40 interviews, with inconclusive results, as it quickly became a matter of one person's word against another's. Superintendent Brown was not allowed to terminate the Schmidts, whom he felt were troublemakers, but there was no specific action taken against

Jacob Duran, the school's Native American disciplinarian, or the superintendent himself.

Continued complaints brought another government investigator to Phoenix in 1930, again with inconclusive results, although this investigator was suspicious of the Schmidts' motivations. The Indian commissioner cleared the school but warned against the disciplinarian's continued use of slapping and flogging. The Schmidts next took their story of excessive discipline, including the alleged 1922 death of one Yuma Indian boy after severe punishment, to the newspapers. John Collier, then executive secretary of the American Indian Defense Association, gave speeches and wrote articles condemning the rampant practice of flogging and incarcerating American Indian students.

The resulting U.S. Senate investigation revealed that the Yuma Indian boy ran away from school a month before he died in a local hospital from meningitis, not from a beating. Other allegations of brutal floggings could not be verified. It is perhaps unfortunate that this issue became so highly politicized and sensationalized, because there was undoubtedly some truth to the allegation that inappropriate physical discipline occurred at Phoenix Indian School, even after the government's mandate to abolish corporal punishment. However, this issue degenerated into an unprofessional feud between the Schmidts and the superintendent. Superintendent Brown, one of the old guard who believed in corporal punishment, was called before the Senate Subcommittee of Indian Affairs in 1931 to testify, and his inability to explain why his school graduates could not compete and find jobs, as well as his defense of the old ways, led to his forced retirement. In the clash between the reformers and the Indian boarding school establishment, the old guard came up losers.

Health Issues at the Phoenix Indian School

Beginning with Carlisle, the Indian boarding schools all struggled with health issues. With a large number of children confined together under less-than-sanitary conditions, the spread of disease was rampant and difficult to contain, and too many children were sent home to die. The biggest culprits were tuberculosis and trachoma at most of the Indian boarding schools, and Phoenix Indian School was no exception. The situation became so serious that in 1908, the Smithsonian Institution and the Indian Office sent Dr. Aleš Hrdlička to the Phoenix Indian School to investigate. Due to its dry climate, Phoenix had become a haven for people suffering from respiratory diseases, and tubercular patients congregated in tent camps that surrounded the Indian school during the winter.

Phoenix Indian School became a test site for health improvements that would subsequently be instituted at other off-reservation boarding schools. Dr. Hrdlička first eliminated the swimming tank, which the school used for recreation and bathing, and substituted shower baths. The school was removed from septic tanks and placed on the city's sewer system, individual towels were issued to the students, lavatories with running water were installed, and attention was paid to the laundry, with the dorm laundry separated from the hospital laundry. Even the mouthpieces of the band instruments had to be sterilized before they changed hands. The Phoenix campus built its own hospital, so that the sick students could be removed from the general school population. The East Farm Sanatorium was established in 1909, when three patients were removed from the school area to a farm the school owned on the outskirts of town. By 1911, there were 84 tuberculosis patients in permanent facilities at the East Farm Sanatorium.

Congressional funds were used to establish an eye clinic on the campus in 1909. The eye specialist discovered that approximately 75 percent of the students suffered from some form of trachoma, a painful eye disease. The clinic was kept busy by treating both students and other Native Americans from the local reservations. The hundreds of cases addressed in the first year eventually dwindled so that the regular school physician could handle all new cases beginning in 1912. The facilities increased and permanent medical personnel were assigned to the sanatorium, and soon it began admitting tubercular patients from other Indian schools and from the surrounding reservations.

Many Native American boarding schools eventually had to build their own hospitals on site, in order to separate the ill children from the others in the dorms, as diseases spread so quickly. Phoenix was typical in this, although it received much attention because of the size of the school, as well as its situation in Arizona, which became a haven for tuberculosis patients throughout the country. Eventually, as the diseases were better understood and controlled, and as the boarding schools became smaller or nonexistent, the hospitals were closed. By the 1950s and 1960s, the Indian boarding schools no longer had on-campus hospitals and utilized local community hospitals.

Changing Political Climate: 1950s and 1960s

By the 1950s, Phoenix was a high school with a residential campus for Native American students, like many of the other former Indian boarding schools. Approximately 700 Native American students attended the high school, and most of them were local students from the southwestern tribes, making it the largest off-reservation government boarding school of this era. It is not surprising that Phoenix Indian High School flourished, since the state of Arizona contained more Indian reservation land than any other state. The pendulum had swung once again toward vocational training, and a local newspaper article asserted that "the Indian School now is simply preparing its graduates to earn a living in industry right here in the community, instead of returning them to the reservation where the economic outlook is bleak" (Trennert, 1988, p. 211). The girls took classes in typing, cosmetology, waitressing, and retail sales while the boys took more academic classes in math and science. Phoenix Indian School was responding to the postwar government programs to relocate returning Native American soldiers into the cities instead of having them return to the reservations. Students were also being trained for city jobs, not reservation jobs, and the boarding school curriculum was revised to provide enough academic rigor so that graduates could go on to higher education. It became government policy to try to funnel students away from the economically blighted reservations.

In 1960, the school officially became Phoenix Indian High School (PIHS) when it gained accreditation by the North Central Association of Colleges and Secondary Schools, and the curriculum was brought up to the standard of other public high schools. PIHS was also affected by the political climate of civil rights in the 1960s, and a new interest in ethnic identity was soon reflected on the PIHS campus. Lee Brightman, the director of the American Indian studies program at the University of California, Berkeley, visited the high school in 1970 and again in 1972, sparking an interest in ethnic identity, and fanning the flames of the "hair controversy" at the high school, with male students becoming interested in wearing their hair long and in braids as an expression of their Indian identity.

The general unrest in society at large was reflected at the school. Students began demanding rights of all sorts, including the right to not do homework or attend classes. Interest in "red power" led to campus unrest and disruption in classes and protests in the cafeteria. Discipline became an issue and many of the school's traditional activities and events were no longer of interest to the students. However, membership burgeoned in the tribal clubs and interest in exploring their ethnic identity was strong among the students. As problems continued, the school was fenced in to help contain the students.

The growing dysfunction of the school became public, which again raised the issue of the purpose of the school and whether it should be continued.

By this point, many Indian boarding schools had already closed. Those that remained open survived only because the Native American population that they served stepped forward to advocate for their continuation. The U.S. government was more than willing to close down all Indian boarding schools, now administered by the Bureau of Indian Affairs (BIA). This new willingness smacked of termination, the government policy that sought to cut loose all Native Americans as government dependents. The termination policy was crafted to address the issue of the continued relationship between the U.S. government and its Native American citizens as a colonial and dependent relationship. But on a practical level, such a move would remove the debt and the benefits owed by the government to the Native Americans as a result of past treaties signed and allow the government to shirk its responsibilities to the Native American nations destroyed in military takeovers.

Thus, in a topsy-turvy scenario, the Native American parents fought to retain the very schools they once fought against. In the past, their children were forcibly put in the schools to be assimilated into the enemy society and to also act as hostages for their parents' cooperation with the government. Now, the Native Americans wanted to retain the schools that were a part of their history and heritage and which they had "Indianized" over the years. They sought to retain and control the boarding schools and make them over to serve the needs of the Native American communities.

At the close of the 1960s, government improvements to rural areas and reservations made local schools even more accessible, and the trend was even more pronounced for Native American students to attend local public or reservation schools. Increasingly, Phoenix Indian High School, as well as other government boarding schools, became a dumping ground for Native American students with social problems or learning disabilities, who were unable to adjust to mainstream schools. In addition, it offered an educational environment that emphasized a Native American–based curriculum, unlike local public schools. Some students continued to report being more comfortable in an all-Indian environment, as prejudice against Native Americans in public schools during the 1950s and 1960s was pronounced.

Phoenix Indian High School: The End

During the 1970s, many of the traditions that symbolized the Phoenix Indian High School were discontinued, in an era of change when many traditions were being questioned. The Nativity Pageant, which had been produced annually at Christmastime as a large community event in Phoenix since the early 1940s, was discontinued in 1972. Perhaps it was not surprising that this symbol of Christian Western culture was finally rejected as irrelevant by the Phoenix Indian High School students. It was in 1973 that the traditional open house day, given annually to welcome the families of the students, changed its name to Indian Day, although the day's activities remained substantially the same. The 1970s also saw the beginning of a new tradition: the election of Miss PIHS, a beauty queen representing the school and the Native American idea of beauty.

In 1980, a local alternative newspaper published an article that described the severe problems with alcoholism at the school, and reported that school sex parties and tribal gang battles were affecting nearby Phoenix neighborhoods. The students reacted angrily in their own articles printed in the school's newspaper, *The Redskin*. During the same year, a federal bill was passed to encourage retirement, and 12 senior Phoenix Indian High School educators, including the principal and vice-principal, left the school. During the following year two former students filed suit against the school for being expelled without a hearing. This suit was symptomatic of a school in trouble; during the 1984–85 school year, 256 students out of 700 were expelled "for vandalism, substance abuse, violence, cutting classes, and related anti-social behavior" (Parker, 1996, 56–67).

In 1985, the Bureau of Indian Affairs sent out a team of educators to investigate matters at Phoenix Indian High School and report back. Their findings indicated that the school had totally failed its students. Multiple problems were documented, including the lack of face-to-face teaching time, with many students working out of printed workbooks and cassette units instead of attending class. There were also large amounts of unsupervised free time on campus from 3:00 P.M. to lights out, with few staff members available for supervision and fewer activities available—even the school library was closed. The academic, vocational, and residential staff had little intercommunication, and school leadership was lacking. The following year, enrollment dropped by 200 students; new high schools were scheduled to open on the Hopi and Tohono O'odham reservations, which previously sent students to PIHS. As a result of the situation, the principal was relieved of duty and a new one appointed, but there were few people who did not see the end of the school coming. Again, it was the Phoenix business community that decided the school closure would be best, just as that group originally advocated for the school's opening. The simple reason was that PIHS sat on the largest tract of undeveloped, commercially valuable land in the center of the city of Phoenix, which was booming. Enrollment dropped to 109 students, and plans were made that the class of 1990 at PIHS would be its last.

Various business and governmental entities gathered to dispose of the PIHS land long before the graduating class of 1990, consisting of 19 students, marched for one last time to the strains of "Pomp and Circumstance," and received their high school diplomas. The Native American community's concerns were practically an oversight until late in the negotiations, even though it was their school, and many had fond memories of it. There were two concerns that arose from the Native American community, one of which involved the preservation of some of the PIHS historical buildings, and a way to preserve what was essentially a part of their history. The most pervasive concern, however, involved the unvoiced mandate for the PIHS students. They wanted a place that would provide vocational training and professional help for the troubled students, reasoning that newly opened reservation high schools would not have such resources or capabilities.

The resulting deal, finalized in Public Law 100-696 and signed into law by President Ronald Reagan in 1988, allowed a commercial developer to have 68 percent of the land for development, in trade for land that would eventually become the Florida Panther Wildlife Refuge and the Ten Thousand Islands Wildlife Refuge, and a $35 million trust fund administered by the Inter Tribal Council of Arizona for the purpose of educating Native American children in grades 1–12. Ten percent of the land went to the Veteran's Administration for an expansion, as they were located next door to the school. Eighteen percent of the land went to the City of Phoenix for an urban park, and the remaining 4 percent was deeded to the State of Arizona. Today, the Steele Indian School Park in downtown Phoenix (opened in 2001) provides 75 acres of open space in the middle of the city. Of the three remaining historic Indian school buildings, only the Memorial Hall has been renovated. Its grand opening in 2008 heralded a venue for community performance and meeting groups. The old dining hall (1901) will be renovated in the future to provide space for a Native American cultural center, and the old band building (1933) is slated to become administrative offices. Steele Indian School Park also boasts a dog park, amphitheater, neighborhood park, and the American Indians Veterans Memorial site. Phoenix residents enjoy their annual Fourth of July fireworks display in this park.

References

Parker, Dorothy R. *Phoenix Indian School: The Second Half-Century.* Tucson: University of Arizona Press, 1996.

Sekaquaptewa, Helen. *Me and Mine: The Life Story of Helen Sekaquaptewa as Told to Louise Udall.* Tucson: University of Arizona Press, 1969.

Trennert, Robert A. "'And the Sword Will Give Way to the Spelling-Book': Establishing the Phoenix Indian School." *Journal of Arizona History* 23 (spring 1982): 35–58.

Trennert, Robert A. "Corporal Punishment and the Politics of Indian Reform." *History of Education Quarterly* 29, no. 4 (winter 1989): 595–617.

Trennert, Robert A. "From Carlisle to Phoenix: The Rise and Fall of the Indian Outing System, 1878–1930." *Pacific Historical Review* 52 (1983): 267–91.

Trennert, Robert A. "Peaceably if They Will, Forcibly if They Must: The Phoenix Indian School, 1890–1901." *Journal of Arizona History* 20 (autumn 1979): 297–322.

Trennert, Robert A. *Phoenix Indian School: Forced Assimilation in Arizona, 1891–1935.* Norman: University of Oklahoma Press, 1988.

EIGHT

Native American Education in the 20th Century and Beyond: Self-Determination, Education, and the Fate of the Boarding Schools

Contemporary Native American Boarding Schools

MANY BOARDING SCHOOLS were established by the U.S. government in the late 1800s with the intention to assimilate Native Americans into the predominant European American culture. Education was a secondary goal; the primary goal was to "civilize" the Native American children, by eradicating their own language and culture and substituting the English language, Christian religion, and the European American work ethic. On the two coasts of the United States, the main difference in their approaches was dependent upon how recently they had fought Native Americans as enemies. On the East Coast, educators thought that the Native American children could be the equal of European American children, if they were removed from their culture and the degrading influence of their homes and families. Educators in the western United States felt that the Native Americans were less capable intellectually than European Americans, and that the primary reason for educating them was because it was a less expensive way to keep the peace with the Indians than financing an army to kill them. Although this philosophy seems wrong and horrifying in the 21st century, these were the ideas that resulted in the birth of the Native American boarding schools, which have played a significant role in U.S. history.

Throughout the succeeding years, the flavor of the Indian boarding schools changed slowly, responding to changing political and cultural trends in the country, although always backward in the way of entrenched institutions staffed by government employees for whom change was not attractive. The initial pattern of Indian boarding schools being half educational and half vocational, and mostly self-supporting, was a pattern that remained unchanged for decades. The militaristic roots of the Native American boarding schools continued long past their usefulness; Indian children dressed in uniform and marched to classes and mess halls until the 1930s. Many schools progressed on individual paths, but most were torn between providing vocational training and an academic education throughout their institutional lives. Some schools swung dramatically between the two, such as Haskell, which at one point became a vocational school, only to metamorphose again into a college; an institution of higher education, which none of the original boarding schools was ever intended to be.

Federal educational policy changes came fast and furious for everyone in the 20th century, and the Native American boarding schools that survived were substantially changed. The new educational policies created a climate that encouraged the growth of tribally controlled schools, spanning elementary education through college. Existing side by side with these new schools are the remaining residential boarding schools run by the Bureau of Indian Affairs (BIA). There are few of them now, and those that continue to exist do so because of Native American support. Rather than a school for Native American students to learn to be white, today's boarding schools celebrate and support Native heritage. They offer more educational opportunities around native culture than most local public schools offer, and they often serve as high schools of last resort for troubled Native American students.

Recently, a group of Native American students at the Sherman Indian High School in Riverside, California, advocated for a place for the Indian residential boarding school in 21st-century America. While the early Indian boarding schools sought to destroy American Indian culture, the contemporary schools are supported by Native Americans. The boarding schools, such as the former Sherman Institute (established 1903), currently promote Native American culture by offering courses on Native American languages, history, arts, and culture, which cannot be found in most community public high schools. The students often come from families who have attended the same boarding school for generations and take comfort in following a family tradition. While their grandparents may have been forced to attend a boarding school, today's students seek to have the experience of being educated with other Native Americans at a residential facility away from home. Some boarding school residents may live on remote rural reservations, and for them, the boarding school is a way out, a more appealing alternative than long bus rides to a rural school where being a Native American is not appreciated.

Mentioned by many of the students at Sherman Institute is the fact that all of the students are Native American, and what a comfort and an excitement it brings to meet similar people from many different tribal backgrounds.

This is one aspect of boarding school life that has not changed over the decades. New friends are made, relationships built, and leaders are born. "Contemporary off-reservation boarding schools are a product of a power change, one that is intended to be of positive value to American Indian students" (Dixon, 2006, 236).

The historical by-product of Native American boarding schools, that of forming a pan-Indian network, still exists in contemporary boarding schools. Sherman Indian High School has contemporary stories of inter-tribal marriages and of alumni moving into tribal leadership positions, even in the 21st century. Contemporary Native American boarding schools are residential high schools that are valued and supported within the Native American community.

Federal Educational Policy

There were multiple American education and social policies that shaped the changes during the latter half of the 20th century:

Meriam Report (1928): In 1926, a team of investigators was given the task of investigating and analyzing the state of affairs of Native Americans in the United States by the secretary of the interior. Their work was external to the government, and was funded by the Rockefeller Foundation. In the resulting report, published two years later, one section was devoted to education, in which the investigators emphasized the importance of education in order to assimilate Native American children into American society. An examination of the off-reservation boarding schools run by the federal government was extremely critical and condemned the overcrowded conditions of the institutions, the poor diets, and poor medical care. The team also took exception to the practice of using student labor to support the boarding school. This report ultimately resulted in a shakeup at the Indian Bureau, closure of some boarding schools, and changes in both conditions and curricula in other boarding schools. It heralded the Indian New Deal.

Indian Reorganization Act, or, Indian New Deal (1934): Also known as the Wheeler-Howard Act, the primary purpose of the Indian Reorganization Act was to end the practice of allotment, in which the government took communally owned reservation land and allocated parcels of land to tribal members to own individually. In this manner, thousands of acres of land owned by tribes under treaties made with the U.S. government was lost. The act also sought to apply the educational reforms recommended in the Meriam Report to improve the boarding schools, provided for Indian religious freedom, set up the first steps for tribal self-government, and allowed for Indian ethnic preferences in hiring Indian Service employees.

Johnson-O'Malley Act (1934): This act allowed the federal government to contract with states to subsidize education in public schools for Native American students, because Native American families pay no taxes that support public education. This was one piece of legislation that eased the stranglehold of the Bureau of Indian Affairs on each aspect of Native American life, and encouraged Native American students to enroll in local public schools. Largely as a result of this legislation, 65 percent of all Native American children in school were attending public schools in 1970 (Szasz, 1999, 89). While this legislation had the effect of curbing the rapid growth of Indian boarding schools when it was passed, its major effects occurred over time, and it proved to be a major influence on education through the 1950s, 1960s, and 1970s.

Kennedy Report (1969): In 1967, a Senate subcommittee, led by Senator Robert F. Kennedy, was formed to examine and study Indian education in the United States. The resulting Kennedy Report was issued in 1969 under the auspices of Senator Edward Kennedy, who finished the work after his brother's assassination. This report was severely critical of federal government policy, stating that the government's policy of coercive assimilation had worked to the detriment of the education of Native American students. The report accuses the academic failure of government-run, off-reservation boarding schools as contributing to the cycle of poverty within Native American communities.

The report's recommendations included holding a White House Conference on American Indian Affairs, creating a national board of Indian education, and increased funding to several existing educational programs. Further, the report recommended not terminating any services to American Indians without their consent. This report made an impact on Native American education, as boarding schools scrambled to respond to the criticisms with improvements. During the 1970s, federal funds were made available for the physical improvements to several boarding schools. The Chemawa Indian Boarding School campus major remodeling project was completed after the report was issued.

Indian Education Act (1972): The Nixon administration responded favorably to the Kennedy Report and appointed Louis Bruce (a Mohawk-Sioux) as commissioner of Indian Affairs. During his tenure, a major piece of legislation was passed, which put the concept of self-determination into action. The Indian Education Act provided supplemental funds for Native American students in both on- and off-reservation schools. Used to redress some of the problems outlined in the Kennedy Report, Part A of the act provided that disbursing the aid funds required parent and community participation, thus delivering the first strike for self-determination. It further stipulated that 10 percent of the funds were supposed to be allotted to schools that were not local public schools, which encouraged the establishment of community schools. Part B established grant programs for culturally relevant and/or bilingual curriculum materials for students. Part C provided grant funding for adult education projects for Native Americans, with a preference for projects generated by Indian tribes or organizations. Part D established a new federal bureaucracy, the Office of Indian Education, located in the U.S. Office of Education and headed by a deputy commissioner for Indian education to be selected from a list of nominees submitted by the all-Indian National Advisory Council on Indian Education. Part E established funding for teacher training for government-run Indian schools, again with a preference for Native American applicants.

Native American Languages Act of 1990: This legislation rejected the historic policy of the U.S. government to eradicate Native American languages and affirmed the rights of tribes to establish their native language as the official tribal language. In many ways, this legislation reaffirmed the bilingual educational practices that arose during the 1960s and responded to the English-only policies that arose in many states since the 1980s.

Indian Nations at Risk Task Force Report (INAR 1991): The 1983 report about American education in general, entitled "A Nation at Risk," laid the groundwork for a further assessment of Native American education six years later by the secretary of education. A 12-member task force consisting of key Native American educators, held regional hearings, made school visits, gathered testimony at special issue sessions of the National Indian Education Association's annual conference, and commissioned papers from selected key educational specialists. The result was a report titled "Indian Nations at Risk," which was as shocking as the initial task force report on American education in general. The report listed four reasons that Native American students were at risk: The failure of schools to educate large numbers of Native American students, as evidenced by high dropout rates; the discouragement of native language use, leading to language loss; the diminished land base of the Native Americans, and the fact that Indian self-determination was challenged by constantly changing policies, rules, and court cases.

The paper went on to list 10 goals for Native American education: early childhood education programs for Native American children; a multicultural school environment and an opportunity for native language maintenance; literacy in English; academic achievement equivalent to other students; high school completion and graduation (lower dropout rates); high quality school personnel; alcohol-free, drug-free, and safe schools; available vocational and lifelong learning opportunities; restructured schools; and parental, community, and tribal partnerships to enrich the educational program.

White House Conference on Indian Education (WHCIE 1992): The White House Conference on Indian Education took place in Washington, DC, on January 22–24, 1992. The purpose of the conference was twofold: first, to explore the possibility of an independent board of Indian education that would oversee all federal educational programs for Indians, and second, to develop recommendations for the improvement of existing Indian educational programs. Before the conference took place, however, individual state steering committees held pre-conferences, which involved Native Americans, educators, and tribal and state leaders at the broadest local level to examine issues locally. Two hundred and thirty-four conference delegates convened and built on the work of the local pre-conferences.

For the Native Americans who felt that this was just another conference that would be a waste of time, the outcomes were refreshing. The broad base of participation at the local level was honored by the conferees, who were mostly Native American. They rejected the idea of an independent board overseeing all federal education, feeling that this diminished tribal sovereignty and added another layer to the existing federal bureaucracy. The delegates utilized the results of the state meetings in order to craft 113 resolutions designed to improve Indian education. The resolutions could be categorized into 11 major topics, beginning with governance of Indian education. The conference came firmly down on the side of local governance of schools, rejecting the idea of a national board.

Further resolutions were made to strengthen the role of the Native American community in education, to make long-term funding of educational programs available, and to increase the retention and graduation rates of Native American students. Resolutions promised safe, alcohol- and drug-free campuses, appropriate education for students with disabilities, and a comprehensive early childhood program that ensured readiness for school for young Native Americans. Strengthened support for native languages and culture was the topic of several resolutions, as was additional support for tribally controlled colleges and financial aid for Native American students attending post-secondary institutions in general. Adult education and lifelong learning were addressed in the conference resolutions, and local control and determination of student needs were a major theme of many of the resolutions. The conference delegates were concerned with comprehensive and holistic services for Native American students, because the piecemeal efforts of government agencies, while well-intentioned, too often fell short in providing adequate educational experiences. Another major theme was to provide a higher quality of standards and services and ensuring fairness and accountability in the educational action plans.

Results of Educational Self-Determination

After the White House Conference, there was little movement on national Native American education issues, and Native Americans had to fight continually to get the federal government to recognize their trust responsibilities and to fund Native American educational programs. In 1995, the Office of Indian Education was practically voted out of existence, and Native American frustrations with having to fight for educational budgets, which were being slashed, continued until President Bill Clinton issued Executive Order 13096, which established six goals for the improvement of American Indian and Alaska Native education in 1998. The goals were to improve reading and mathematics, increase high school completion rates, reduce poverty and substance abuse, create strong, safe, and drug-free school environments, improve science education, and expand the use of educational technology. These goals were bolstered by a 2001 General Accounting Office study that found that the performance of students in BIA-funded schools fell far below the performance of students in public schools, even though more dollars per pupil was spent.

In 2000–2001, the BIA Office of Indian Education Programs was operating 65 schools, while the tribes were operating 120 schools. These schools were located in 23 different states, with most in Arizona, New Mexico, North Dakota, South Dakota, and Washington. From the 1970s onward, Native Americans enrolled in institutions of higher education in increasing numbers, higher than at any time in history. In 1995, Native Americans represented 0.8 percent of all U.S. college students. In three institutions of higher education, Native Americans formed the entire student body—Haskell Indian Nations University, Southwest Indian Polytechnic Institute, and the Institute of American Indian Arts.

Haskell Indian Nations University, an institution that continues to be governed by the Bureau of Indian Affairs, was originally begun in 1884 as one of the original Native American boarding schools. The historic campus currently hosts approximately 1,000 Native American students who are working on degrees in American Indian studies, environmental science, business administration, and elementary education. Its extremely low graduation rate in 2010 gained it a poor reputation. In its heyday, Haskell had the top football program in the United States.

Southwest Indian Polytechnic University is a tribally controlled college that opened in 1971, governed by the All Indian Pueblo Council in Albuquerque, New Mexico. It offered two-year community college certificates for direct employment and transfer degrees, but lost its accreditation in 2010.

The Institute of American Indian Arts was chartered by executive order of President John F. Kennedy in 1962. Located in Santa Fe, New Mexico, it offers two- and four-year degrees in museum studies, creative writing, visual communications, indigenous liberal studies, and studio art. With an enrollment of approximately 250, the IAIA alumni include some well-known artists and authors. The campus also houses the noted Museum of Contemporary Native Arts.

In the late 20th century, the new notable trend in Native American education became the tribally controlled colleges, something not heretofore seen on the American higher education landscape. "In their 30 years of growth the tribal colleges have become the institutional cultural intermediary for Native college students, reaffirming Native identity and the training for survival in the contemporary world" (Szasz, 1999, 235). The first tribally controlled college was Navajo Community College (now Diné College) established in Arizona in 1968. The impetus and leadership for this college had its seeds in a unique program that began earlier on the Navajo reservation, called the Rough Rock Community School.

Rough Rock Community School

From 1950 to 1965, the main focus of the BIA Branch of Education was to increase school enrollment, because it was evident that thousands of Native American children had no access to education in the 20th century. Consequently, there existed little support for the concept of community schools, although it was an idea that made sense to everyone. The Navajo Nation, which currently encompasses 27,000 square miles in a remote part of the country spanning three states, was due to have a new boarding school built on the reservation. The chairman of the Tribal Education Committee, Allen D. Yazzie; Robert Roessel, an educator from Arizona State University; and others convinced the Office of Economic Opportunity to fund an experimental school run by the Navajos instead of building the boarding school.

The Rough Rock Community School began in 1966 near Chinle, Arizona, and stood as the only example of self-determination in education for many years. The constant stream of visitors and the publicity garnered by the pioneer program added to the issues that the school needed to deal with. The school came from the community, was embedded in the community, and was used as an economic stimulus for the community. Navajo culture was a key part of the curriculum. Statistics show that its academic strength was sacrificed for community strength, because its students compared poorly with another BIA boarding school on the reservation.

The Navajo Curriculum Center, founded in 1967 with additional grant funds, found its home in Rough Rock and began the vital work of turning an oral tradition into written curriculum units of Navajo history and culture, to be added into school studies on the reservation. A 1969 external review of the Rough Rock Community School, led by Donald Erickson, found that the school had no set curriculum and that the school's priorities were primarily funding and publicity, secondarily providing jobs for local Navajos, and third was everything else, including curriculum.

At the edge of Black Mesa, Arizona, a large water tower declares "Rough Rock" in block letters and at its feet sits the elementary school campus: the school itself, employee houses, dormitories, cafeteria, clinic, plant management services building, and two large hogans—one is the Navajo Studies Center and the other accommodates community cultural activities. Rough Rock opened its doors on September 12, 1966, to 220 students, first through sixth grade. "This is a community-oriented school, rather than child-oriented," stated Robert Roessel to a visiting reporter (quoted in McCarty, 2002, 84). The fact that this Navajo-controlled school was led by an Anglo principal, Robert Roessel, created some conflict, and, ultimately, Roessel left to act as the first president of Navajo Community College, the nation's first tribally controlled school of higher education.

Rough Rock's short-lived Navajo Curriculum Center made major contributions to bilingual and bicultural Navajo literature, still in use today, and addressed the greatest problem and greatest need of the new school: the complete lack of Navajo texts and Navajo-English bilingual materials. Of the many community development programs started at Rough Rock, the Navajo Mental Health Project probably had the most positive impact and survived the longest. After the first flush of spending federal grant money to begin such community programs as a greenhouse, poultry farm, and furniture factory, which quickly failed, the community learned how to administer its educational programs in a more savvy manner.

The Navajo community discovered that controlling their own educational institutions was not easy, and where federal funds were involved, so were grants, reports, and evaluations. Starting the program with only three certified Navajo teachers, the school originally hired outside teachers and paired them with Navajo teaching assistants. They quickly determined that they needed to "grow their own" certified Navajo teachers, and over the succeeding years did so successfully with a series of programs and grants. The Navajo teachers were change agents, and were key contributors to the school's success and longevity. Self-determination brought with it the responsibility for quality control, and Rough Rock Community School was the first of many tribally controlled educational programs. The tribe learned it had to develop its own educators and support for the school as much as it relied upon the school to act as a source of jobs for the community.

Based largely on the Rough Rock experience, the BIA began to promote bilingual education in the 1960s and 1970s. In addition, several new federal initiatives made it possible for education to be placed under local control in that era. The possibilities promised by the Rough Rock Community School could now be made real by other Native American communities. Rough Rock ran teacher preparation classes and more classes to teach written Navajo to its teachers.

The 1980s were Rough Rock's middle years. After the heady excitement of breaking new ground, the reality of the long haul set in. Fluctuating and unreliable funding, teacher turnover, and dropping enrollments began to plague the school as it prepared to seek accreditation after 20 years of operation. During the 1980s and the accompanying Reagan administration, much of the grant-based federal funding dried up and the community-based schools faced the possibility of closure. Two elements that weighed in favor of the school's success were that they built a local, bilingual faculty, and they were successfully accredited by the North Central Association in 1992, which ensured federal funding.

The 1990s saw community conflict, protests, allegations of mismanagement, and a boycott that tore the school apart. In 1997, Robert Roessel returned after 31 years to help Rough Rock pull itself together and renew their commitment as a community-based, bilingual school. He stayed for two years to stabilize the school and recharge the Navajo studies program. The community reaffirmed its goal to have their students educated to function in two languages and in two worlds.

Today, the newest threat to Rough Rock is the current obsession with national educational standards, which have a monolingual and monocultural bias and have a completely chilling effect on a bilingual, bicultural program that has proven so effective in the past. Teachers are being forced to teach to standards and shortchange their Navajo program. The educational consequences of the national standards movement remain to be seen.

Rock Point Community School

Another community school, also located within the Navajo Nation, transitioned gradually from a BIA-run school to a community-run school and began with English as a second language (ESL) classes in 1960. Initially, its students ranked lowest in the standardized tests among the BIA-run schools. The students improved their ranking to the top of the BIA schools, but were still below standard compared to all other schools. In 1967, a bilingual program was initiated using grant funds, and this expanded, when a local school board was elected in 1972 and contracted with the BIA to run the school. In order to get and keep enough qualified teachers for the classes taught in Navajo (43 percent of the students were dominant Navajo speakers in 1988), the teachers were hired locally without college degrees but were provided funding to receive their appropriate degrees. Completing a college degree was a condition of their continued employment, and every teacher but one completed this requirement. Many of the teachers created their own materials in Navajo, and the school continued to teach reading and math in both Navajo and English; students also turned in writing assignments in both English and Navajo. In 1983, the eighth grade Rock Point students outperformed all other Native American students in the state of Arizona on standardized tests. Not only were the test scores good, but the school succeeded in so many other ways: Student attendance rates were high, parents were involved in the school, and the students improved and refined their Navajo language skills as they learned English and content matter.

Navajo Community College (Diné College)

Given the existence of the previously mentioned educational programs, it is no surprise that the first Native American-controlled institution of higher education was also born in the Navajo Nation. In 1968, Navajo Community College was funded by the Office of Economic Opportunity (OEO), the government office leading the War on Poverty; the Navajo Tribe; and the Donner Foundation. Strongly supported by Navajo Chairman Raymond Nakai, the Tribal Education Committee worked diligently to get this groundbreaking project underway, with classes being held in 1969 at a BIA high school in Many Farms, near the Rough Rock Community School. In 1971, construction began on a permanent campus located on land donated by Yazzie Begay at Tsaile, Arizona. The first college president was Robert Roessel, former director for the Center of Indian Education at Arizona State University and former director of Rough Rock Community School. The time was ripe for a Native American college; and even the BIA, which opposed the Rough Rock Community School project, was on board with the new Navajo Community College.

Of course, there were different visions for the new community college. Traditionalists wanted the college to act as a tool to preserve and transmit traditional culture, while other tribal members hoped the college would prepare Navajo students to transfer to mainstream four-year colleges or equip them to enter the job market. In 1971, the U.S. Congress passed the Navajo Community College Act, which provided federal support for the college. One of the key components of the new community college was its Navajo Studies program, which provided a unique Navajo curriculum.

The first tribally-controlled college in the United States was Navajo Community College, established in 1968. Now known as Diné College (Tsaile, Arizona) the institution continues to blend the old and the new, with Navajo culture embedded in the school's architecture and curriculum. (NativeStock Pictures)

Mainstream college courses were also offered, but were taught from a Navajo point of view. Although the college began with an Anglo president and 40 percent Anglo faculty, the Anglos were given no voice in the college governance and direction, which was guided by an all-Navajo Indian Council and Board of Regents. The college's second and subsequent presidents were all Navajo, and the Anglo teachers were replaced as soon as qualified Navajo teachers became available.

The college's mission became preparation of students for two different paths. For those students intended to transfer to a four-year college, a curriculum was developed to meet those transfer requirements and was supplemented by the Navajo Studies courses. The philosophy was that the students who went into the outside world most needed to understand their own history, culture, language, and identity. For those intending to find work on the reservation, the college offered vocational courses such as nursing, secretarial training, auto mechanics, welding, and so on. The old vocational programs taught at the boarding schools were always out of date and unrelated to jobs available on reservations; at last, the Navajos controlled the skills taught in school in order to match them with available reservation jobs.

Navajo Community College was accredited by the North Central Association of Colleges and Schools in 1976, and is now a multicampus institution serving the 27,000 square mile Navajo Nation, which spans the three states of Arizona, New Mexico, and Utah. In 1997, Navajo Community College changed its name to Diné College, to better reflect the peoples' name for themselves, and established the school's philosophy of balance and harmony, with four guiding principles of thinking, planning, living, and assuring.

In 1973, leaders of NCC and five other tribally controlled colleges formed a national organization called the American Indian Higher Education Consortium (AIHEC). Their first action was to attempt to secure guaranteed funding from Congress, and their efforts led to the passage of the Tribal College Act (1978). In 1988, they established the American Indian College Fund, a large pool of private funds, and in 1994 the AIHEC was again instrumental in the congressional award to tribal colleges of land grant institution status, which aids in funding. The organization persists in 2011, with 23 member institutions.

Federal Educational Policies

In 1997, Senator Ben Nighthorse Campbell, the only Native American senator, became the chair of the Senate Indian Affairs Committee, laying the groundwork for the Comprehensive Federal Indian Education Policy Statement, which had been in draft form since 1995's Education Summit. Its roots went back to the Indian Nations at Risk Report of 1991 and the White House Conference on Indian Education of 1992. After much widespread input from the nation's Native American educators and legislative revisions, President Bill Clinton signed the long-awaited Executive Order on American Indian and Alaska Native Education in 1998, culminating years of work. Even though in 1997, 89 percent of K-12 Native American students were enrolled in public schools, the effect of the order would be to ensure that public schools incorporate some native curriculum elements in a respectful manner.

Finally, with the new trends in Native American educational policy and with the establishment of tribal-run institutions of higher education, the locus of control for native education is moving back to where it belongs: with the Native American community. We may begin to see the type of education that Luther Standing Bear imagined, a place where Native Americans learned from the Anglos, and where the Anglos also learned from the Native Americans, for the betterment of both and for the betterment of the land that we now share. The Native American students are able to have an educational experience that is not designed to strip them of their language, culture, and identity, but one that is designed to reinforce their native culture. As Luther Standing Bear said in 1933:

> To the end that young Indians will be able to appreciate both their traditional life and modern life they should be doubly educated. Without forsaking reverence for their ancestral teachings, they can be trained to take up modern duties that relate to tribal and reservation life. And there is no problem of reservation importance but can be solved by the joint efforts of the old and the young Indians. . . . Why not a school of Indian thought, built on the Indian pattern and conducted by Indian instructors? (Standing Bear, 1933, 252–54)

References

Diné College: The Higher Education Institution of the Navajo Since 1968. http://www.dinecollege.edu.

Dixon, Patricia, and Clifford E. Trafzer. "The Place of American Indian Boarding Schools in Contemporary Society." In *Boarding School Blues: Revisiting American Indian Educational Experiences,* edited by Clifford E. Trafzer, Jean A. Keller, and Lorene Sisquoc, 232–42. Lincoln: University of Nebraska Press, 2006.

"Haskell Indian Nations University." *Wikipedia.* http://en.wikipedia.org/wiki/Haskell_Indian_Nations_University.

"Institute of American Indian Arts." *Wikipedia.* http://en.wikipedia.org/wiki/Institute_of_American_Indian_Arts.

McCarty, Teresa L. *A Place to Be Navajo: Rough Rock and the Struggle for Self-Determination in Indigenous Schooling.* Mahwah, NJ: Lawrence Erlbaum, 2002.

Reyhner, Jon, and Jeanne Eder. *American Indian Education: A History.* Norman: University of Oklahoma Press, 2004.

Southwestern Indian Polytechnic Institute: A National Indian Community College and Land Grant Institution. http://www.sipi.edu.

Standing Bear, Luther. *Land of the Spotted Eagle.* Lincoln: University of Nebraska Press, 1933.

Szasz, Margaret Connell. *Education and the American Indian: The Road to Self-Determination Since 1928.* 3rd ed. rev. and enl. Albuquerque: University of New Mexico Press, 1999.

NINE

Boarding School Legacy

THE CHAPTER IN AMERICAN HISTORY OF USING EDUCATION, specifically off-reservation government-run boarding schools, as a means to eradicate native languages and cultures and to assimilate native students into the dominant European American society is a misguided, shameful, yet vital piece of American history. Prior to their boarding school experiences, whether the students were forcibly taken to school by the authorities or forced to go by parental decree or willingly asked to go, each student had already experienced years of indigenous education within their family and community. Even as they lived away from their people, learning a new language and a new way of life, they still held their previous experiences at their core.

While many of the children were open to adding new experiences, languages, and customs to their personal repertoire, they tended to take what was useful or attractive to them and quickly discard what was not. In many institutions in the early years, students speaking their own languages was forbidden, as was wearing their traditional clothes or expressing their own culture. Such actions merited harsh punishments. Yet groups of students managed to escape the watchful eyes of matrons in order to converse quietly in their own tongues, create their own playthings based on remembered culture, and share stories. True, many times the stories were told in English, as it was the common language among the children, who came from many different native cultures. Historic photographs show girls playing on the grassy grounds of a boarding school with a miniature camp, complete with tiny tipis and miniature horses pulling travois and larger dolls carrying baby dolls in cradleboards. Personal accounts of boarding schools tell of groups of boys dashing into nearby woods with handmade bows and arrows to practice shooting and teaching each other remembered stories and dances. According to scholar Dr. K. Tsianina Lomawaima, native cultural expressions gradually became tolerated in the boarding schools, as long as they did not challenge the status quo or challenge the subservient political position of the Native Americans in society. The safety zone theory accounts for the presence of Native American language and cultural artifacts in institutions dedicated to their eradication.

In addition to the shock of entering the boarding school, the shock of finding others like them and yet not like them was another element to adjust to. Without caring adults around, peer groups became important, and the students looked out for each other, if they were not bullying each other. But the students were not helpless lumps of clay to be molded by the teachers at the boarding school. They each came with their own education and experiences, and they accepted and rejected various parts of their boarding school experiences based on their own needs and desires. The outcome or result was different for each and every student.

Social Implications of Institutionalization

One of the social issues examined by *They Called It Prairie Light* was the effect of total institutionalization on students' ability to think and act independently. As with many other outcomes of the boarding school experience, the students experienced different, even conflicting, results from the same institutional system. Some students, after being raised in a boarding school where they were told what to do and when to do it, every minute of the day, and their days were organized for them so that they changed activities at the sound of a bugle or bell, had difficulties making decisions and establishing their own routines and self-discipline after they left boarding school. One of the alumni interviewed, Juanita (not her real name) said, "It was very hard when I left there because there were no schedules, there were no bells ringing and no whistles blowing: I didn't know what to do. And I didn't do very well. . . . And nobody told me where to be at a certain time. There was no schedule made up; you had to do it yourself. And it's hard" (Lomawaima, 1994, 122).

Conversely, the school's dependence upon student labor created situations where upperclassmen often needed to take leadership positions in order to teach the younger students. The military organization at the school resulted in some of the students being given leadership positions and being placed in command of companies of younger students. Older students in the trades often bore the responsibility of getting projects done and teaching younger students in the trades. Lomawaima observes, "Trades instructors spent most of their time directing the older students, the juniors and seniors, who in turn directed the younger students. Senior boys directed work in the print shop, butcher shop, power plant or farm; girls assisted the dormitory matrons or the physical education instructor; both genders excelled on athletic teams; officers served in the military system. Within these 'niches of responsibility' students developed important qualities: independent thought, independent action, a sense of responsibility, leadership, and self-sufficiency" (Lomawaima, 1994, 123).

These outcomes were unplanned by the boarding school educators and were inconsistent; based on each student's circumstances and experience. An examination of individual student case studies shows that some students were unable to take independent action after growing up in a boarding school, while others were almost overequipped with a sense of duty and responsibility and a capability for independent action. As with so many of the boarding school outcomes, the results were totally unplanned and unexpected and varied widely among the students.

Homecoming: Ambivalent Student Responses

For the boarding schools and for the students themselves, the ultimate test of the value of their boarding school education happened when they returned home for good. "Returned students" represented a topic of concern for their European American educators from the beginning and were studied and theorized about through the years. Memoirs and letters written by the students provide some insight into their return to the reservation, and like all other aspects of the boarding school experience, their return home and their future lives varied widely according to the individual.

The great fear of the educators, that students would return to the reservation and live their old lives as if they had never attended school, going "back to the blanket," in the rude language of the times, was one result that happened more often than not, certainly more often than the European American educators hoped for. Many returning students found that there was nothing gained by their education that could be used at home on the reservation. They saw the world of school as one world and the world of home another, with different rules, dress, and language, and no interaction between the two worlds. A great many students simply passed from one world to another after they left school.

In many ways, the students who simply returned to their former place in society were probably the lucky ones. There are stories of students not welcomed home, rejected by families and friends for being changed and different. There were those students who believed in the superiority of the European American education they acquired and who were rude and insensitive to their family and community members upon return, rejecting their families and homes. Michael Coleman's book, which is based on the autobiographical accounts of boarding school students, gives many examples of less-than wonderful homecomings. Shawnee student Thomas Alford wrote, "My homecoming was a bitter disappointment to me," after graduating from Hampton Institute (Coleman, 1993, 178). He was not welcomed home with open arms, but rather with suspicion and coldness. He looked different, acted differently, and scorned many of the aspects of his new daily life, comparing them unfavorably with boarding school. Returning Hopi students Helen Sekaquaptewa and Irene Stewart found it difficult to live again in dirt-floored hogans lacking hygienic facilities. For all of the difficulties of boarding school life, they and other returning students found that the grinding poverty of daily traditional life was difficult to readjust to. The boarding schools, in their zeal to make over their Native American students into the image of white America, ignored one very basic fact of life: After leaving boarding school, their students had to go home. The students needed to be prepared to live in two cultures, not one.

Many students had a difficult time after homecoming, but eventually made their own way without a guide, because they were the new cultural mediators, the ones who understood European American society enough to interpret it for the others in their traditional community. For Helen Sekaquaptewa, who admittedly was uncomfortable in her parent's hogan upon return, it is perhaps symbolic that she and her husband lived on the edge of the reservation in her own home where she created her own blend of cultures. Her traditional sister, who despised Helen's new habits and routines, took over her traditional dwelling. Others, such as Zitkala-Sa (Gertrude Bonnin) were unable to reconcile with their family and find meaningful jobs in their home communities, and left their reservations forever, returning to the European American world to live and work. Zitkala-Sa dedicated the rest of her life to activism, promoting the interests of all Native Americans.

Still other boarding school graduates were able to return home and find a place in their own communities, which allowed them to make use of their education and to earn a respected place in their societies as a cultural intermediary. It is documented that quite a few of the boarding school graduates became tribal leaders, equipped as they were by language and knowledge of the European American world to represent their own communities in negotiations with the U.S. government. Luther Standing Bear occupied a position of trust among the Sioux, running a dry goods store at Pine Ridge, and later, Ivan Sidney and Peterson Zah, both Phoenix Indian School graduates, became tribal leaders in Arizona.

Leo Crane, a Hopi agent, addressed the so-called failure of boarding school returnees at length in his government reports. He commented that,

Zitkala-Sa (Dakota) exemplified the direction that many boarding school graduates took. She taught at Carlisle, was a lifelong activist for Native American rights, and founded a pan-Indian organization, the National Council of American Indians, in 1926. (Library of Congress)

first, the students discovered that their industrial training was useless. Of what use is a carpenter on a desert reservation with no wood, or a shoemaker in a community where everyone makes their own moccasins? The student had to adjust to his home community or leave. Yet, Crane suggests, the schooling did make an impact. "In actuality, white schooling usually left a decided imprint on students. More often than not, returned students were able to converse in English, desired the luxuries and conveniences of modern life, were more attuned to hygiene, were more suspicious of old superstitions, and would see the advantage of education for their offspring" (Adams, 1995, 300). Crane went on to describe the so-called failure of boarding school graduates as a failure because the returned student "is not what the taxpayer expected him to be. He is not what the faddist and sentimentalist tried to make him" (quoted in Adams, 1995, 300).

The success or failure of a returned boarding school student was something heavily debated and studied at the time. It was a revelation to everyone that the individual students were not passive vessels, simply soaking up new information. They participated actively in learning about a new culture, and learning new information. Most students selectively adopted that which was useful to them and fit it into their own world view. Some rejected everything that they learned. The results and outcomes sought after by the studies could not be categorized or calculated. Each student adapted to his or her circumstances in a unique way and created their own future.

Returned Student Survey

In 1916, the Board of Indian Commissioners sent a survey to the various superintendents of Indian agencies, asking them to identify the reasons for the failure of the returned students. Aside from the fact that the board was probably surveying the wrong population, the answers varied widely. Indian agents listed various reasons for returned student failure, such as lack of community support, poor morals, natural laziness, and the fact that trades learned at boarding school did not match reservation needs. Leo Crane, the Hopi agent, addressed this issue in a clear and thoughtful manner (see above). Other agents questioned whether the returned students could be called failures at all.

One frustrated, overworked Indian agent responded this way to the survey: "I have no suggestions about the Indians. I think they are doing very well indeed, everything considered. But I have a deep-seated grouch against an overwhelmingly large number of Caucasians who are not living up to their opportunities. A Board should be organized to investigate them"

(Frank Virtue, Superintendent, Tule River Indian Agency, Porterville, CA, 1918. *Ayer MS 907*, vol. 4, Newberry Library, Chicago).

Formation of a Pan-Indian Consciousness

Another unexpected by-product of the boarding school experience was the formation of a pan-Indian consciousness. Each student who wrote about their boarding school experience mentioned the unity and solidarity formed with fellow students who supported each other through the educational experience and acted as a substitute family at boarding school. Certainly, the fact that the students were thrown together in a strange environment, enduring traumatic times together, generated strong bonds between the students. Few of the boarding school memoirs dwell on the academic subjects learned, but many mention the friendships and sharing with friends and how rich and meaningful it was for the students. Casual get-togethers where students shared songs and stories were described. Gathering to hunt in the woods, cook a stew over a fire or parch corn—these represent very fond memories of the participating boarding school students. Thus, the students gained an appreciation for each other's culture, recognized something similar, yet unique about the Native American cultures they came into contact with, and formulated strong friendships.

While the original purpose of the boarding school was cultural genocide and began with the use of English only for instruction and interaction within the boarding school, Sally J. McBeth's dissertation asserts that the use of English stimulated pan-Indianism. Originally, the boarding schools were formed to strip away a student's tribal identity, but in recent years, Native American boarding schools have come to represent "Indianness" and to promote a Native American identity. This has been expressed by Native American opposition to the closing of Indian boarding schools. Contemporary Native Americans argue that these schools represent the federal government's treaty obligations to the tribes and should be maintained. Also, in the quest to maintain their identity, the Native American boarding schools now are the educational institutions that most strongly nurture that cultural identity.

School sports were mentioned often as an activity where the male students worked together, had fun, and were able to beat the white students at their own games. Several Native American boarding schools became national sports powerhouses, beginning with Carlisle. Sports represented an area where the students succeeded. However, in the formation of a pan-Indian consciousness, hard lessons had to be learned. Students tended to associate with others from their own tribal group at boarding schools, and often tribal gangs experienced conflict. Playing sports broke down tribal rivalries and promoted pan-Indianism. At Phoenix Indian School, where the football team consisted of linesmen from one tribe and running backs from an enemy tribe, the students had to choose between protecting their traditional enemies or losing to a white school.

Dr. Lomawaima notes that the pan-Indian identity was forged in solidarity among the students resisting the institutionalization of the boarding schools. Resistance took many forms, from running away to playing tricks on teachers or simply sneaking out to eat candy and talk together after lights out.

Students from tribes that had never interacted were thrown together and given a common language (English) with which to communicate and a common "enemy" (the school) to oppose. In addition to giving the students a new network of friends, years spent at a coeducational boarding school often led to intertribal marriages, much less common in the past. Esther Horne, a Shoshone from Wyoming, married a Hoopa Indian from California, and they continued working at Indian boarding schools, she as a teacher and he as a staff member. How did the lesson of pan-Indianism play out in actual life after students left school? Just as it is no surprise that many tribes drew their leaders from the boarding school students, it is also no surprise that boarding school students formulated key pan-Indian political and social organizations and have actively used them in order to pursue benefits for their own communities. In banding together, they have been able to achieve that which they could not have achieved separately.

Probably the first pan-Indian organization, the Society of American Indians (SAI), was formed in 1911 by Native American professionals, many of them boarding school graduates. A moderate and progressive organization, they were not allowed on the campus of the Phoenix Indian School. The SAI was not radical enough for Zitkala-Sa, so she founded the National Council of American Indians in 1926 for the purpose of helping Native Americans interact with the Bureau of Indian Affairs and to help them secure their rights in regards to property and citizenship. She worked as an independent reformer on Indian-related issues and her skills in public speaking and her knowledge of the BIA, results of her life as a boarding school student and teacher, helped her to help others. This pan-Indian organization gave her a platform for her activism, and she served as its president until her death.

Today, a whole host of pan-Indian organizations, in which Native Americans from different tribes gather in order to promote the benefit and welfare of their individual cultures and communities, remains an unexpected legacy of the boarding school era. Currently, the National Congress of American Indians (NCAI) works to protect tribal sovereignty, and has been doing so for the past 67 years. The American Indian Higher Education Consortium (AIHEC) has been instrumental in the creation and support of our nation's tribally controlled colleges. These organizations are one legacy of the students that are described by anthropologist Malcolm McFee as the "150% man" (McFee, 1968). His study of Native Americans on a bicultural reservation led to the conclusion that for some individuals, acquisition of a new culture is not balanced by an equal loss of traditional culture. Such individuals are adept in two cultures, thus the appellation "150% man."

Tribal Colleges

Another outcome of the boarding school educational movement was logical—tribal colleges—given the changing educational climate. The original boarding schools educated Native American students first at an elementary school level, later at a secondary school level. The students were being educated to work in American society, even though the original intention was for the work to be menial in nature, it is not surprising that many of the students looked toward higher education. Native American students inspired by their own Native American teachers and students who had part-time or outing jobs in local businesses decided to attend college in order to do the work of their choice.

Native American students have struggled to compete in public colleges and universities that may be far from home. In the new era of self-determination, it was possible for tribes to establish institutions of higher education that created educational opportunities for their youths right at home, so they did not have to move far away. Many of these schools were better equipped to educate their students in a culturally acceptable and accepting manner, preparing them in the best way to work in the local community.

Persistence of Native Language and Culture

From the beginning, the stated primary purpose of the Indian boarding school was not to educate, but to erase the student's native culture and to replace it with the dominant European American culture. Colonel Richard Henry Pratt, founder of Carlisle Indian School, the first off-reservation government boarding school, is credited with often saying "kill the Indian, save the man" as a description of his educational philosophy. In an 1899 speech about Pratt, Commissioner of Indian Affairs W. A. Jones remarked, "It was understood that unless the Indian youth be educated and assimilated

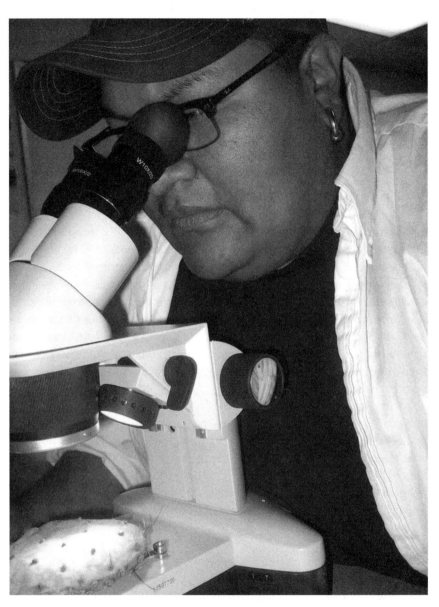

One response to government-controlled boarding schools has been for tribes to take control of their own educational institutions. Today, a student at the Tohono O'odham Community College (Sells, Arizona) peers through a micro-scope in a biology class. (Melissa Silver/American Indian College Fund)

with our population, the tribes would stand as a menace to the peace of the government and require a large army to keep them within bounds" (Quoted in Reyhner, 2004, 143). The early students at Carlisle were as much hostages to their tribes' peaceful intentions as anything else, and Pratt sought to eliminate their use of their own language and erase cultural markers with a missionary zeal. As time went on, the purpose of the boarding school did not change, but the harshness of the cultural genocide abated with time.

Whether harsh and explicit, or implicit and subtly undertaken, the goal to eradicate Native American languages and cultures had limited success from the beginning. Even though the Native American students were removed from their homes and placed far away, so that there was little to no interaction with family, and even though severe punishments were meted out for speaking their native language, the students went home after three years. If they chose to live in their home community, they spoke their native language after that, unless they had some use for the English language. There was a documented language loss among the indigenous tribes after European contact, but this can be attributed to a combination of factors, including education. Proximity to English-speaking communities and work opportunities in English-speaking workplaces, military service, intermarriage, broken families, and general poverty are all factors that contributed equally to language loss, in addition to English-language education. In recent years, there has been a resurgence in native language learning among many different tribes.

Although the boarding school students may have gained a sense of pan-Indian solidarity, at bottom, they never lost their ethnic identity. Indeed, in some instances the boarding schools served to reinforce Native American cultural identities. Urban Indians who attended boarding school not knowing their language or culture, reported learning tribal cultural elements at boarding school for the first time, and they certainly became aware of other students' languages and cultures, to the extent that they shared with one another. Many boarding school memoirists say that they "learned what it is to be Indian" at the boarding schools, and that this was its greatest gift and most lasting legacy.

Students as Cultural Mediators

There is little doubt that the boarding school students have served as cultural mediators, or translators, between the Native American and European American cultures. Boarding school graduates abound in the ranks of tribal governing officials, Bureau of Indian Affairs employees, educators, and teachers. Luther Standing Bear ultimately became an actor representing Native Americans on the big screen and struggled to have Indian roles given to Native Americans. Zitkala-Sa published stories about Native American traditional tales and of her life experiences, as did other boarding school graduates, adding their voices to the American scene. Using their knowledge of English and the dominant culture, the early boarding school graduates became doctors, lawyers, artists, writers, soldiers, businessmen, and politicians. They contributed by working to give Native Americans a voice in America, while simultaneously working to retain their sovereignty, their culture, their language, and their land.

Healing

Dr. Eulynda J. Toledo is a second-generation boarding school survivor, and believes that many of the current social ills in Native American society can be attributed to the intergenerational trauma caused by boarding schools. She founded the Boarding School Healing Project to help boarding school survivors heal themselves and seek justice. They are looking to the international human rights arena and the United Nations as avenues to seek justice and reparations for abuse and oppression experienced at boarding schools.

A $25 billion class-action lawsuit was filed against the U.S. federal government in 2003 for the physical, sexual, and psychological abuse suffered by the Native American claimants while attending boarding schools, but was subsequently dismissed. In Canada, the last of the First Nations boarding schools was closed in 1984, and in 1998 the Canadian government apologized to First Nations boarding school survivors and set aside funding for counseling as a reparation. There is a sense that this chapter has not yet reached closure in the United States.

Just the Beginning

It is only within the past decade that much of the scholarship about Native American boarding schools has been published. There is still much work to be done; much more to be written on this topic. We still need to hear from many more boarding school students about their experiences at school, whether it was 50 years ago or last year that they graduated. We need more information about the mundane details of dorm life, and we need to know how the school changed over time.

We need to have more information about running away and discipline. And we need to know more about a dark and secret topic hovering in the shadows—sexual abuse. It was not addressed in this book due to a dearth of published materials, but it is certainly there. When the outing girls of Phoenix Indian School were sent to private homes unescorted as domestics, what happened to them? How did they cope? A boarding school system that was criticized for poor health conditions in the dorms probably did not have protections against sexual predators.

But we also need to increase our information about the positive aspects of boarding school life. The accounts we have illustrate the importance of friendships and of Native American role models and mentors. Some memoirs praise the stability of the boarding school system for children from broken, dysfunctional homes and dangerous communities. There were tricks, pranks, and jokes. There were escapades and secret feasts and treats. All of this information is necessary for us to see the complete picture of the Native American boarding school era in U.S. history.

References

Adams, David Wallace. *Education for Extinction: American Indians and the Boarding School Experience, 1875–1928*. Lawrence: University Press of Kansas, 1995.

Ayer MS 907, vol. 4. Chicago: Newberry Library, 1918.

Boarding School Healing Project. http://www.boardingschoolhealingproject.org.

Coleman, Michael C. *American Indian Children at School, 1850–1930*. Jackson: University Press of Mississippi, 1993.

Colmant, Stephen, Rockey Robbins, and Lahoma Schultz. "Constructing Meaning to the Indian Boarding School Experience." *Journal of American Indian Education* 43 no. 3 (2004): 22–40.

Lomawaima, K. Tsianina. *They Called It Prairie Light: The Story of Chilocco Indian School*. Lincoln: University of Nebraska Press, 1994.

McBeth, Sally J. *Ethnic Identity and the Boarding School Experience of West-Central Oklahoma American Indians*. Dissertation, 1982, Washington State University.

McFee, Malcolm. "The 150% Man, a Product of Blackfeet Acculturation." *American Anthropologist* 70 no. 6 (December 1968): 1096–1107.

Parker, Dorothy R. *Phoenix Indian School: The Second Half-Century*. Tucson: University of Arizona Press, 1996.

Pember, Mary Annette. "A Painful Remembrance." *Diverse: Issues in Higher Education* 24 no. 21 (2007): 24–27.

Reyhner, Jon, and Jeanne Eder. *American Indian Education: A History*. Norman: University of Oklahoma Press, 2004.

Zitkala-Sa. *American Indian Stories*. Lincoln: University of Nebraska Press, 1985. Originally published Washington: Hayworth, 1921.

Short Biographies of Key Figures

Elias Boudinot (Cherokee)
(1804–1839)

Elias Boudinot was born in Oothcaloga in the Cherokee Nation, in what is now northwest Georgia, the son of Cherokee warrior Oo-watie (David Watie) and Susanna Reese, the daughter of a Cherokee woman and white trader. Originally named Galagina, which translates to "Buck" in English, Buck Watie attended the Moravian mission school in the Cherokee Nation, then applied to the American Board of Commissioners Foreign Mission School in Cornwall, Connecticut. While traveling to Connecticut to begin school, Watie's traveling party stopped to visit Elias Boudinot, the American Bible Society founder and a great believer of American Indian equality. When he registered for school in Connecticut, Watie chose the name "Elias Boudinot" as his adult name. He believed, as did the original Elias Boudinot, that if he learned and accepted the European American way of life, he would be able to live as an equal in Euro-American society. Subsequent events proved just how wrong he was.

Boudinot was an excellent student and a convert to the Christian faith. He was joined at the Foreign Mission School by his cousin, John Ridge, who became very ill. During his illness, Ridge met the daughter of his nurse, Sarah Northrup, and they fell in love and got married. This rocked the small Connecticut town, and the unfavorable reaction it provoked caused Elias Boudinot to put a hold on his burgeoning romance with the physician's niece, Harriet Gold, whom he met during his cousin's illness.

Boudinot returned to Cherokee country to serve as the clerk of the Cherokee council for two years, but in 1826, he embarked on a lecture and fund-raising tour of the large cities in order to acquire the funds to start a Cherokee newspaper in the Cherokee language, recently invented by Sequoyah. During that same year, he returned to Cornwall and married Harriet Gold. This second interracial marriage created such an uproar, that Harriet feared for her life, and she fled her home and hid in the house of

133

a sympathetic neighbor. The scandal created by their marriage caused the closure of the mission school, and Harriet joined her husband in the Cherokee Nation capitol, New Echota. Elias taught school to earn money, and continued his quest to start a Cherokee newspaper. His belief that American Indians and European Americans could live together as equals was shaken. He hoped that the Cherokees could build a separate but equal nation within a nation.

Ultimately, Boudinot's efforts were successful; the Cherokee council purchased a printing press and type, and named Elias as the founding editor of the bilingual, biweekly *Cherokee Phoenix*. The first issue of the paper was published in 1828. The *Phoenix* reprinted translated news from other papers, but it also acted as an official organ of the Cherokee Nation, printing the laws and public documents of that body, along with opinion columns written by the editor. Boudinot wrote on various topics, ranging from the evils of alcohol to the insatiable thirst of their European American neighbors for land and gold. The state of Georgia sought to extinguish the Cherokee claim to their land and boldly offered lands within the Cherokee Nation up for lottery.

In *Worcester v. Georgia* (1832) the U.S. Supreme Court found in favor of the Cherokee Nation, but President Andrew Jackson refused to enforce the decision, and white intruders continued to flood into the Cherokee Nation to rob and threaten the Cherokees. Through the tenor of Boudinot's editorial columns, it became clear that he believed that the only solution was to sign a treaty with the United States and remove to the West with other tribes. However, the official policy of the Cherokee Nation was against removal, so Boudinot was not allowed to air discussion of this issue in the newspaper, although he felt it to be important news. This conflict led to Boudinot's resignation from the *Cherokee Phoenix* in 1832, and he continued to work politically to find a solution to this pressing issue.

Harriet Boudinot died in 1835, after giving birth to the couple's sixth child. Boudinot was grief stricken and during that year became involved in signing the Treaty of New Echota. The treaty relinquished the Cherokee lands in Georgia for different lands in Oklahoma and precipitated the forced removal of the Cherokees to the west under horrible conditions, resulting in more than 4,000 deaths. This treaty was not supported by the Cherokee council, but it was accepted by the United States because it gave them what they wanted. Boudinot, his new wife, and children left Georgia for Oklahoma, and settled in Tahlequah, the capitol of New Echota, to become immersed in the work of translating the Bible into the Cherokee language. Elias Boudinot was executed by an unknown group of Cherokee men in 1839 for violating a Cherokee Nation law that prescribed the death penalty for any Cherokee who illegally signed a treaty resulting in the loss of Cherokee land.

Adam Fortunate Eagle (Ojibwa)
(1929–)

Born Adam Nordwall in 1929 to an Ojibwa mother and Swedish father, Adam was sent to Pipestone boarding school at age five with his four siblings after his father died, leaving the family in dire financial straits. He grew up at Pipestone Indian Training School and avoided the most severe effects of the Great Depression. After graduation from Pipestone, he attended Haskell Institute in Kansas, where he met his future wife Bobbie, a Shoshone Indian.

The Nordwalls moved to San Francisco in 1951, where Adam worked as a termite inspector and eventually owned his own company. He soon became active in a local Native American group, the United Bay Area Council of American Indian Affairs, and in 1969 he proposed the takeover of Alcatraz Island. While some regarded this as no more than a publicity stunt, it did get wide press coverage, and as a result of focusing attention on Native American issues, is often regarded as the beginning of the "red power" movement.

Nordwall's termite business filed for bankruptcy in 1975, after government scrutiny revealed code violations, the outcome being assessment of fines. These, coupled with the IRS audit that resulted in back taxes, put Nordwall out of business. It is speculated that the intense government scrutiny might have been due to his activism; most of the other activists were students with nothing to lose, but Nordwall had a home, family, and business.

At age 42, Nordwall was gifted with the Indian name of Fortunate Eagle, which he embraced and has used since that time. After leaving San Francisco, Fortunate Eagle and his wife moved to her home on the Paiute-Shoshone reservation near Fallon, Nevada, where he has lived as an artist, author, and activist. There he practices the calumet pipe-making that he learned while at Pipestone, along with creating traditional headdresses. In 1987, Fortunate Eagle was arrested for selling protected eagle feathers to an undercover fish and wildlife agent, and continues to pay fines for that transgression. Also a traditional dancer and lecturer, he received the Governor's Arts Award in 1996.

Fortunate Eagle is the author of *Pipestone: My Life in an Indian Boarding School* and is the subject of a documentary entitled *Contrary*

Warrior: The Life and Times of Adam Fortunate Eagle. Depending on who you ask, he is either a publicity stunt-seeking embarrassment, or a coyote trickster who raises awareness with his "serious joke medicine."

Reverend Samson Occom (Mohegan) (1723–1792)

The son of Joshua Ockham and Sarah Sampson, Samson Occom was born in a Mohegan village near New London, Connecticut. He was converted to Christianity at age 17 and became known as the Pious Mohegan. Through his mother he was related to Uncas, a well-known Mohegan leader, and his father's father was Tomockham (Ashneon). His mother was also a Christian convert and influenced Samson to enroll in Eleazar Wheelock's Indian Charity School in 1743 at Lebanon, Connecticut. Gifted with languages, Samson learned English, Greek, Hebrew, and Latin and later taught Oneida.

Poor health plagued him his entire life, and he was unable to transfer to Yale and took a missionary position in New York instead, late in 1749. He was sent by Wheelock to preach to the Montauk Indians on Long Island, where he also acted as their schoolmaster and legal adviser until 1761. He married one of his students, Mary Fowler, in 1751 against Wheelock's wishes, but their union continued until his death, and the couple had 10 children. Occom became an ordained minister in 1759, but was given a miserly 15 pounds per year for his services. When he discovered that European-American ministers were paid more, he bitterly resented that he and his family lived in poverty most of their lives.

Inspired by his success with Samson Occom, Wheelock decided to seek funds to expand his school, and in 1765–68, Occom and another minister, Reverend Nathaniel Whitaker, went to Great Britain to solicit funds for his school. Reverend Occom preached more than 300 sermons throughout the British Isles, and he and Whitaker returned with more than 12,000 pounds with which to start Dartmouth College. Occom believed that the funds were to be used to found a school for the Indians; indeed, this is what all of the donors believed. It quickly became apparent that Wheelock's new college was primarily for European American students, with a nod to the American Indians, few of which attended the institution of higher learning. Furthermore, while Occom was away fund-raising for Wheelock, his family lived in such poverty that his wife needed to beg Wheelock and others for funds in order to survive. This estranged the two men, and their relationship never recovered, as Reverend Occom believed that Wheelock used the funds he raised fraudulently, and they did not benefit the American Indians directly, as was his intent.

Reverend Occom also used his education and his command of English to side with his tribe in the Mohegan Land Case, or Mason Controversy. As early as 1764, the Indians and the settlers disagreed on land settlement rights, and the expertise Occom used to defend his tribe ultimately angered his superiors, and he very nearly lost his license to preach. Unfortunately, the court case got caught up in the Revolutionary War, and along with the British, the Mohegans lost their lands.

Although Occom kept a diary, his entries are prosaic and describe the minutiae of his daily life. But in 1772, he was asked to preach a sermon prior to the execution of another Indian, Moses Paul. His execution sermon, *Sermon at the Execution of Moses Paul*, is one of the best pieces of gallows literature produced during the era and was reprinted many times, going through at least 19 editions. In this first work published in English by a Native American, Occom expounds on the evils of alcohol to the Indians and warns them away from it.

Disillusioned with the European Americans he had encountered, Reverend Occom met with other Christian Indians and planned to found Brothertown, a town established on land in New York donated by the Oneida Indians and populated by Christian Indians who came together from many different tribes. He moved there in 1791 but died a natural death in 1792. For all of his education, he lived an impoverished and hardworking life. Today he is regarded as one of the founding fathers of Brothertown, which was eventually removed to Wisconsin territory. The descendants of the Brothertown Indians are petitioning the U.S. government for recognition as a tribe.

Colonel Richard Pratt (1840–1924)

Born in Rushford, New York, in 1840, Richard Henry Pratt's parents moved to Logansport, Indiana, when he was six years old. A few years later, his father left to join the gold rush but was murdered and his gold hoard stolen. His mother raised the family, and as the eldest son, Pratt began to work at chores at age 10. At age 13, he left school to become a printer's devil and began to work full-time. He answered President Abraham Lincoln's call and enlisted in the 9th Indiana Volunteer Infantry in 1861, just shy of his 21st birthday. He continued to reenlist, and fought in the battles of Nashville and Chickamauga, advancing from a private to a brevet major as a volunteer. In 1864, he was sent home to Indiana to recruit for the army, and there met Anna Mason, who he married before his assignment ended and was sent back to the front lines. Pratt was honorably discharged in May 1865.

After returning home and working for two years in the hardware business, Pratt reenlisted in the regular army in 1867. As a second lieutenant, he was sent to Fort Sill in the Oklahoma Territory with the 10th U.S. Cavalry, a group of freed slaves known as Buffalo Soldiers. He spent eight years posted in the Oklahoma and Texas area and participated in the conflicts with the Native Americans. His western posting was hard on his wife and family, and when he was detailed to accompany some of his American Indian prisoners to Fort Marion in St. Augustine, Florida, he requested a transfer and remained in charge of the Native American prisoners at Fort Marion starting in 1875. During the next few years, the soldiers guarding the warriors were replaced by some of the Native Americans themselves. Uniforms were issued to replace worn clothing, classes in English were taught by townsfolk, and many of the Native Americans were able to find work polishing shells, packing oranges, and doing other odd jobs for money. In 1878, the warriors were released and returned to their western reservations, with the exception of those who requested further education.

Pratt contacted a number of institutions, but they all refused his Native American students, with the exception of Hampton Institute. He went with them to Hampton to supervise the Indian education section of this school for African Americans, but soon petitioned to open a school only for Native Americans on the grounds of the abandoned army barracks at Carlisle, Pennsylvania. He was allowed to do so, but only if he recruited his first students from among the recently defeated Sioux tribes. Pratt opened the Carlisle Indian School in November 1879 with 82 Sioux children. The hallmark of his school was that it was a government-funded boarding school located away from home. The students were immersed in the dominant language and culture and were forbidden to speak their own language or practice their own culture.

Pratt instituted a curriculum of a half day of academics and a half day of vocational training. Because none of his students had previously spoken English, the academic classes were more like English as a second language (ESL) classes and the academic content was at a basic level. The boys learned such trades as carpentry and tinsmithing, and the girls learned basic housewifery. The school fielded an impressive marching band and football team, and during the summers, students were encouraged to participate in the outing program. This program placed students in local homes and businesses to work for a sum of money while they lived with a family.

Pratt believed that the Native Americans would only become assimilated if they were immersed in and participated in the dominant American culture.

Although students were returned home after three years, and Pratt hoped they would continue their education, it is uncertain how many ever did. Despite the questionable outcomes of the Carlisle program, it was enthusiastically embraced and copied throughout the United States and quickly became the norm for educating Native American students. Although his practices are today widely regarded as cultural genocide, at the time he was thought of as an Indian reformer, because he believed the Native Americans to be intelligent and capable human beings, rather than subhuman savages, which was the popular opinion of the time. Pratt was outspoken in his opposition to reservations, believing the segregation of Native Americans from the rest of the populace was contrary to their interests. He denounced the Indian Bureau and riled against the government's civil service system, and was forced into retirement from Carlisle in 1904, after leading the school for 25 years.

He retired to his home in Rochester, New York, where he continued to speak and write in support of Native American causes. Pratt died at the army hospital in San Francisco on April 23, 1924, and was buried in Arlington National Cemetery.

Estelle Reel (1862–1959)

Born in Illinois in 1862, Estelle Reel was educated in Boston and Chicago, then moved to Wyoming to live with her brother, who was mayor of Cheyenne. Estelle worked as a teacher, and in time was nominated to become the Laramie County school superintendent. This was her springboard to further public service, and in 1894 she ran for election as the state superintendent of public instruction as a Republican and won. This victory made her the first woman elected to a statewide office in America. Her campaign tactics excited rumor and comment, as she stumped the state twice accompanied by other male candidates. She admitted that she used the social dances that accompanied the town political meetings to dance with and speak to local Democrats, but denied the damaging story that she sent thousands of lonesome cowboys pictures of herself in order to encourage their votes.

In her new position, she oversaw not only Wyoming's educational institutions, but also its penitentiaries and asylums, as well as serving as the state's land registrar. Her election as the state superintendent of public instruction was seen as acceptable as it related to "women's work," as education was viewed, but Reel's abilities to act as land registrar were questioned. Upon her election, Reel adeptly addressed the key issues of the day, that of creating a standardized curriculum that would be consistent throughout the state's schools, the issue of teacher certification, and the controversy over whether the state should supply free textbooks. Reel was actually very astute about using the lands assigned to the schools in order to increase school revenues through land lease and auction.

During her tenure as the state superintendent of public instruction, Reel equalized the salaries of male and female teachers. This act, and her own position, made her a magnet for suffragettes. Although she was not a radical suffragette, she believed in the women's vote, which was accepted in Wyoming and also in equal pay for equal work. However, she was the first to denigrate the idea of running for state governor, which she saw as a man's job. She remained active in the state Republican Party and campaigned for President William McKinley in 1896, and was credited with being the key to McKinley's Wyoming win. She applied for a federal position and was nominated by McKinley to be the superintendent of Indian schools within the Office of Indian Affairs in 1898. This position required Senate confirmation and was once again a first for Estelle Reel; she was the first woman nominated for such a high government office.

Estelle Reel served as the superintendent of Indian schools from 1898 to 1910, during the period when off-reservation government boarding schools for Native American children were at their peak. Consequently, her policies and decisions affected thousands of young lives. The first thing she did was to tour the 250 government boarding schools, which blanketed the nation and held 2,000 teachers and 20,000 students. It was her responsibility to inspect the schools, hire the teachers, establish the curriculum, and provide the texts. One of her goals was to professionalize the teaching corps, and she endeavored to upgrade the quality of the teachers through judicious hiring and a teacher training program.

The other need that she addressed was one for a standardized curriculum for teaching Native American students. Her Uniform Course of Study was published in 1901 and contained exhaustive, minute details for teaching a large variety of subjects in the boarding schools. Reading her curriculum document exposes Estelle Reel as a racist, in that she believed the Native Americans to be intellectually inferior to Caucasians. She spoke often of the "dignity of labor" and geared the training in the boarding schools toward manual labor for the young men and housewifely training for the young ladies. Her beliefs swung the pendulum of educational policy for Native Americans toward practical or manual labor training. Colonel Pratt's belief that with the proper education, Native Americans could accomplish anything was supplanted with a belief that Native Americans had their (subservient) place in society and should be educated appropriately.

However, Pratt's insistence that Native American languages and culture must be completely eradicated by boarding schools was a position also changed by Reel. She saw no conflict in the inclusion of some Native American arts in her curriculum, which she deemed acceptable and even suggested that skilled elders be hired by the boarding schools to teach weaving, basketry, pottery, and beadwork. These skills conformed to her notions of proper occupations of young ladies. Reel also had a personal appreciation of Native American arts and collected many beautiful examples in her career.

This aspect of Reel's curriculum did not survive past her tenure as superintendent of Indian schools but another innovation did. In her travels, Reel visited the Tuskegee Normal and Industrial Institute, an educational institution for African Americans, in 1906 and borrowed the notion of practice cottages, where a group of senior girls are given a budget and left on their own to manage an actual household for six weeks. The practice cottage concept was imbedded in the boarding school curriculum for years to come. Indeed, Reel's "Uniform Course of Study" and the half day of instruction and half day of occupational training pattern continued in boarding schools until the critical Meriam Report was issued in 1928, and for many schools, it continued beyond that date.

Over the years, Reel suffered from exhaustion and depression; her final years as superintendent were not marked with the enthusiasm and innovation of her early years. In 1910, Congress eliminated the funds for her position and she left office. That same year, she married Cort Meyer, a rancher from the state of Washington, where she moved. She never returned to public service and died in 1959 at the age of 96, living her life quietly out of the public eye in Toppenish, Washington.

Lawney L. Reyes (Sin Aikst/Lake)
(1931–)

Reyes mother was Sin Aikst, now one of the Colville Confederated Tribes, and his father was a Filipino who lived a native lifestyle. Lawney and his siblings, one sister and one brother, lived their early lives on the Colville Indian Reservation in the state of Washington. During 1935–37, they moved to the Grand Coulee Dam construction area and opened a Chinese restaurant with partner and cook Harry Wong. Wong bought out their half of the restaurant in 1937; Reyes's parents separated in 1939 and later divorced. Years later, Reyes's mother would work again for Harry Wong and marry him.

Lawney was a student at Chemawa Indian School near Salem, Oregon, from 1940 to 1942, where he took his first art class and attributes his ideas about being Indian to his interactions with peers at the school. After two years, Lawney returned to live with his father on the Colville Reservation and in Okanogan, Washington, where he graduated from Okanogan High School. He worked his way through Wenatchee Junior College, where he met and married Joyce Meacham (Yakama/Warm Springs) in 1955. He served in the U.S. Army and was stationed in Europe, where he traveled and determined to study architecture, design, and art.

Lawney and Joyce moved to Seattle, where he studied art at the University of Washington, graduating in 1959. Inspired by Pacific North Coast art, he began working in wood, carving three-dimensional pieces. He became a sculptor and was an up-and-coming freelance interior designer and was eventually hired by Seafirst Bank as their interior designer and for whom he worked on various corporate design projects in various locations for 25 years. For his last seven years at Seafirst, he built and was curator of a corporate art collection of some note. During this time, he and his wife had two children, a girl and a boy. His wife's career also grew, and she eventually became the assistant director in the Indian Health Services offices in Portland, Oregon.

Reyes created more than 600 sculptures in his spare time while he worked for Seafirst and gained much recognition and many art awards. He has been asked to teach at local colleges. He took early retirement from Seafirst in 1984 to continue working on his own art, and he also wrote two books. One was his memoir, *White Grizzly Bear's Legacy: Learning to be Indian*, and the other was a biography of his younger brother, Bernie, who became an activist and chairman of the United Indians of All Tribes Foundation in Seattle, Washington, entitled *Bernie Whitebear: An Urban Indian's Quest for Justice*.

Reyes's artwork includes some prominent pieces of public art, such as the sculpture *Blue Jay*, which now hangs at the Daybreak Star Cultural Center, the Native American cultural center for Seattle, which was designed by Reyes. *Dreamcatcher*, another sculpture, located at the corner of 32nd Avenue and Yesler Way in Seattle, honors the memories of his brother and sister. He believes that if the native Pacific North Coast artists had continued their work in an unbroken arc to the present, that their contemporary works would look much like his.

Robert A. Roessel Jr.
(1926–2006)

Dr. Robert A. Roessel grew up in St. Louis, Missouri, where he became interested in Native Americans at a young age. After serving in the Pacific during World War II, he studied anthropology with Robert Redfield at the University of Chicago but forsook anthropology to get his teaching certificate and join the Bureau of Indian Affairs (BIA) as a teacher. He taught on the Navajo Reservation, where he met and married Ruth Wheeler, daughter of a medicine man and a traditional Navajo. They worked together as educators and community organizers. Dr. Roessel worked on obtaining his PhD at the University of Arizona, where he became the youngest full professor on the faculty and founded and served as director for the Center for Indian Education. While at the center, he also established the major scholarly journal for Native American education, the *Journal of American Indian Education.* He also served on a presidential task force for Indian affairs.

In 1966, he was asked by Navajo leaders to work with them to found the Rough Rock Community School, which was the first school governed by an all-Indian board and the first school to teach the Navajo language. Roessel served as the school's principal for the first few years, and the school was widely publicized, studied, and copied. From there, Dr. Roessel went on to found Navajo Community College, now called Diné College, which was the first tribally controlled college in the United States and served as a model for those that followed. He continued to work with the Navajo Nation in a special capacity to fund and establish a tribal museum and responded to the call to return to lead Rough Rock school through troubled times again in 1997. Once the school was stabilized, he stepped down as its director. Dr. Roessel died in 2006, but is widely thought of as an architect of Indian education policy in the late 20th century.

Luther Standing Bear (Sioux)
(1868–1939)

Named Ota Kte (Plenty Kill) upon his birth to Standing Bear and Pretty Face, Standing Bear lived a traditional life on the Rosebud Reservation until his father enrolled him at Carlisle Indian School in 1879, where he was the first student to enter the new boarding school. A Sioux leader, Standing Bear's father had traveled to Washington, DC, and spoken with American leaders. He became convinced that it was necessary for his son to learn about the whites, and sent him east to Carlisle with Colonel Richard Pratt. Standing Bear saw this opportunity as a chance to prove his bravery to his father and the tribe. He attended Carlisle for several years, then worked at a department store. He returned to the reservation to work in his father's trading post and eventually to run a dry goods store on the Pine Ridge Reservation in South Dakota.

In 1902, he served as interpreter for the Native Americans in a wild west show, and he became a dancer and horseback rider for Buffalo Bill's Wild West Show, and turned entertainer, despite the fact that Colonel Pratt would have turned over in his grave at the thought. From there, he went to Hollywood and in 1912 became an actor and helped form the Indian Actors Association with the intent of influencing the studios to hire more Native Americans for their western films.

In the 1930s he published three books about Sioux traditions and his life. He also was artistic and painted pictures of battles, ceremonies, and portraits of Sioux leaders. Although he initially thought of his boarding school education as a positive influence in his life, because he understood the English language and the European American culture, he became less accepting of American culture as he aged, preferring his native culture, and became more critical of the greater European American society. He favored bilingual education and thought that educational institutions should provide a place where European Americans and Native Americans could share culture and learning, rather than a one-way street for turning all students into European American pattern cards.

Zitkala-Sa, or Gertrude Simmons Bonnin (Sioux) (1876–1938)

Gertrude Simmons was born on the Yankton Reservation in South Dakota in 1876, where she lived with her mother in a traditional manner for her first eight years; her father, a white man named Felker, left his family before Gertrude was born. Her mother remarried a man named Simmons, and gave Gertrude his name also. Later in life, at the turn of the century, Gertrude's sister-in-law scolded her for leaving her traditional life and becoming educated, and told her that she must give up her brother's name, since she deserted the family. Gertrude decided to invent her own name, Zitkala-Sa, which means "Red Bird," and used it for the rest of her life.

At age eight, she was lured by the Quaker missionaries with a promise of endless red apples to eat if she went to White's Manual Institute in Wabash, Indiana. She thoroughly disliked the boarding school's "iron routine," and returned home three years later, but found that she didn't enjoy her home life either. A great divide occurred between her and her mother, which would only grow wider through the years. After four years at home, Gertrude, headstrong and independent, decided that her future lay back at school, and against her mother's wishes returned to finish her education at White's, then attended Earlham College in Richmond, Indiana, from 1895 to 1897. At Earlham, she participated on the debate team and had her poems and essays published in the school newspaper. She polished her proficiency in English and used it to express her ambivalence at not belonging in either her mother's world or in the white American world for which her forced acculturation prepared her. She went on to the Boston Conservatory of Music to pursue her studies; she was quite proficient on the violin, and she joined literary societies and began to write.

Zitkala-Sa got a job as a teacher in Colonel Pratt's Carlisle Indian School, and during this time several of her articles were published in *Atlantic Monthly* and *Harper's Bazaar.* She was also briefly engaged to Carlos Montezuma, a Yavapai doctor, during this time. Pratt sent her back to the reservation to recruit students during the summer. She decided to stay and not return to Carlisle. The publication of her stories, which were outspoken against the boarding school system, earned her much criticism at Carlisle. Her intention was to stay on the reservation for awhile, which was rapidly becoming encroached upon by whites, and to record and publish the traditional Sioux stories, which she did right after the turn of the century. While back on the reservation, Zitkala-Sa met Raymond Bonnin, another part-Sioux, and married him. With her marriage in 1902, her literary career came to an end. She and Bonnin had one son, and they moved to the Uintah reservation in Utah, where Raymond obtained a position as a government clerk. Frustrated by her inability to get a teaching position on the reservation, Zitkala-Sa collaborated with William F. Hanson on the creation of the first Native American opera, *The Sun Dance*, which premiered in 1913. She also taught the reservation children music and formed a band.

In 1916, the Bonnins moved to Washington, DC, because Zitkala-Sa was elected secretary of the Society of the American Indian (SAI). Under their umbrella, she began lecturing and working for reforms for all Indians. In 1918–19, she also served as editor for the society's publication, *American Indian Magazine*, and her literary skills were used for a social cause. The organization dissolved in 1920, and Raymond Bonnin went to work as a clerk in a Washington law office, while Zitkala-Sa worked with the General Federation of Women's Clubs to form an Indian welfare committee in 1921. She continued her reform work and spearheaded an investigation into the horrifying crimes surrounding land thefts from Oklahoma Indians who had oil on their lands. Her resulting report in 1924, "Oklahoma's Poor Rich Indians," and her friendship with reformer John Collier, led to the 1928 Meriam Report.

In 1926, Zitkala-Sa founded her own pan-Indian organization, the National Council of American Indians (NCAI) and served as its president until her death in 1938. She used the society to further advocate for reforms and to give a voice to underdog Indians, helping them confront the corrupt agents and intractable Bureau of Indian Affairs. She worked tirelessly with groups of Native Americans to organize their newly won votes and to show them how to become a political force. Outspoken and aggressive, she made enemies, but she never stopped. She was a curious amalgam of sentimentality and drama, juxtaposed against a hard-headed realism that enabled her to operate as a minority female in the world of white male politics.

References

"Adam Fortunate Eagle." *ONE: Online Nevada Encyclopedia.* http://www.online nevada.org/adam_fortunate_eagle.

"Adam Fortunate Eagle." *Wikipedia.* http://en.wikipeida.org/wiki/Adam_Fortu nate_ Eagle.

Bohl, Sarah R. "Wyoming's Estelle Reel: The First Woman Elected to a Statewide Office in America." *Annals of Wyoming* 75 (winter 2003): 22–36.

"Boudinot, Elias." *American National Biography Online.* http://www.anb.org/.

"Elias Boudinot." *About North Georgia.* http://ngeorgia.com/ang/Elias_Boudinot.

"Lawney L. Reyes." *Contemporary Authors Online.* Detroit: Gale, 2008. *Gale Biography In Context.*

"Lawney Reyes." *Seattle Civil Rights & Labor History Project.* http://depts.wash ington.edu/civilr/ reyes.htm.

"Lawney Reyes." *Wikipedia.* http://en.wikipedia.org/wiki/Lawney_Reyes.

Lomawaima, K. Tsianina. "Estelle Reel, Superintendent of Indian Schools, 1898–1910: Politics, Curriculum, and Land." *Journal of American Indian Education* 35, no. 3 (May 1996): 5–31.

McCarty, Teresa L. "In Memoriam: Robert A. Roessel, Jr." *Anthropology & Education Quarterly* 37, no. 2 (June 2006): iii.

McCarty, Teresa L. *A Place to be Navajo: Rough Rock and the Struggle for Self-Determination in Indigenous Schooling.* Mahwah, NJ: Lawrence Erlbaum, 2002.

McManis, Sam. "Profile: Adam Fortunate Eagle Nordwall." *AAANativeArts.com.* http://www.aaanativearts.com/article544.html.

Peyer, Bernd C., ed. *American Indian Nonfiction: An Anthology of Writings, 1760s–1930s.* Norman: University of Oklahoma Press, 2007.

Pratt, Richard Henry. *Battlefield and Classroom: Four Decades with the American Indian, 1867–1904.* New Haven: Yale University Press, 1964.

Reyes, Lawney L. *White Grizzly Bear's Legacy: Learning to be Indian.* Seattle: University of Washington Press, 2002.

"Richard Henry Pratt." *Wikipedia.* http://en.wikipedia.org/wiki/Richard_Henry_Pratt.

"Samson Occom." *American Eras.* Vol. 2. Detroit: Gale, 1998. *Gale Biography in Context.*

"Samson Occom." *Notable Native Americans.* Detroit: Gale, 1995. *Gale Biography in Context.*

Stone, Tammy. "Bonnin, Gertrude Simmons." *American National Biography Online.* February 2000. http://www.anb.org/articles/15/15–00796.html.

Welch, Deborah. "Gertrude Simmons Bonnin (Zitkala-Shaceka): Dakota." In *The New Warriors: Native American Leaders Since 1900* (Lincoln: University of Nebraska Press, 2001): 35–54. *North American Indian Thought and Culture.*

Zitkala-Sa. *American Indian Stories.* Foreword by Dexter Fisher. Lincoln: University of Nebraska Press, 1985.

Primary Documents

U.S. COMMISSIONER OF INDIAN AFFAIRS
REPORT OF THE SUPERINTENDENT OF
INDIAN SCHOOLS

The superintendents of Indian schools oversaw all of the government-run boarding schools in the United States. Their position entailed visiting and inspecting all of the boarding schools, and the annual reports they submitted to Congress contained enrollment statistics and descriptions of the boarding schools. Reading all of these government reports provides a complete history of the Indian boarding schools—from the point of view of the government officials.

The 1901 report was similar to other years, but contained one very important document by then-Superintendent of Indian Schools Estelle Reel. Her Uniform Course of Study (UCS) was included in this annual report, which continued to be utilized by the boarding schools for decades after its inception. This document, issued so that the disparate boarding schools would have a similar curriculum, actually detailed minutely all aspects of instruction for every subject area, and set them in stone. The following are excerpts from the UCS for a couple of subject areas.

Course of Study for Indian Schools

OFFICE OF SUPERINTENDENT
OF INDIAN SCHOOLS,
Washington, August 10, 1991.

**To Agents, Superintendents, and Teachers
of Government Schools:**

An outline course of study for the Indian schools is herewith submitted to you, and I trust it will receive your cordial and active support.

This course is designed to give teachers a definite idea of the work that should be done in the schools to advance the pupils as speedily as possible to usefulness and citizenship.

The aim of the course is to give the Indian child a knowledge of the English language, and to equip him with the ability to become self-supporting as speedily as possible.

Methods of instruction and subjects of study have their limitations in value, and in view of the aims and purposes in educating the Indian, who is just starting on the road to civilization, such methods must be employed as will develop the various powers and capacities with which the child is endowed, and, by systematic industrial training, give him the skill in various directions designed to be service-able in meeting the demands of active life, making him a willing worker as well as an inquiring learner.

The value of education must be measured by its contribution to life interests, and it is our purpose to fit the Indian pupil for life. It is the privilege of the elemen-tary school to awaken the child's capacities and quicken his interests, giving him an appreciation of his own powers, awakening his interest in and appreciation of things about him, cultivating a desire to cooperate with his fellow-men in the pur-suit of knowledge and its achievement.

In this course practical lessons in every branch are outlined. The child learns to speak the English language through doing the work that must be accomplished in any well-regulated home, and at the same time is being trained in habits of indus-try, cleanliness, and system. He learns to read by telling of his daily interests and work with the chalk on the blackboard. In dealing with barrels of fruit, bushels of wheat, yards of gingham, and quarts of milk, in keeping count of his poultry, and in measuring his garden he becomes familiar with numbers in such a practical way that he knows how to use them in daily life as well as on the blackboard in the schoolroom.

It should be the constant aim of the teacher to follow this course and to us much more in each grade as he or she has time to accomplish; but the chief end in view should be the attainment of practical knowledge by the pupil, and no teacher should feel restrained from asserting his or her individuality in bringing the pupil's mind to a realization of the right way of living and in emphasising the dignity and nobility of labor.

As far as possible teach the children that the cultivation of good habits, self-control, application, and responsiveness are recognized as being on a higher educational plane than a knowledge of definitions and unimportant dates; that the development of character is the only imperishable object for which we can work; that consequences follow action with unfailing certainty, and that "it is the purpose that inspires and the motive that holds to our task that limits the extent and value of our service."

Hoping that better morals, a more patriotic and Christian citizenship, and ability for self-support will result from what this course of study may inspire, I am,

Very respectfully,

ESTELLE REEL.
Superintendent of Indian Schools.
Approved:

W. A. JONES, *Commissioner.*

Harness Making

Teach the essential principles that underlie a number of trades and ability to do many kinds of work rather than give the boy a trade. See that he has gained intelligent ideas of tools and their uses, the laws of mechanism, the properties of wood, iron, leather, and other materials. Teach system and precision.

The aim must be to give a more symmetrical education, employing the brain and hand by using books and tools, in order that increased interest in all work and more useful citizens may result.

First Year.—The boy must first be taught to make a war end; then give him scraps of leather to sew upon until he learns to make a good stitch. He will then be advanced to strap work, which necessitates much practice on stitches.

Give plain work, such as traces, folded breaching, bellybands, hip straps and halters. The necessity and value of good, careful stitching cannot be too strongly impressed.

The making of the different kinds of pads used on harness is a very important branch and should be taught carefully.

Talks should be given frequently on leathers of different kinds, where obtained and how tanned, and those best suited for the different parts of the harness; also upon the proper care of harness and the tools and materials used in making harness.

Second year.—Continue the work on straps and give thorough instruction in making bridles. Give also the round work.

Third year.—The work this year involves much practice in cutting and fitting all parts of the harness and in putting them together to complete a full set of harness, and the talks must embrace a thorough study of leather and where to obtain the best grades. Have pupils observe the different kinds and styles of harness. Give practice in estimating cost of leather and all supplies pertaining to the harness trade. Drawings showing the different parts of harness, as well as complete sets of harness for wagons and carriages, will also be made by the pupils from memory as well as from the articles themselves.

History

Begin teaching history by telling the children the story of their tribe and then of their race. Relate to them legends and stories such as will excite and fix their interest. Have the pupil tell what he can of the history of his forefathers and of his tribe as it has been handed down from the fathers and mothers in tales told around the camp fires. The parents have lived through pages of history. Oral and written reproduction of all such historical stories form an important part of the work.

Endeavor to arouse in the pupils an interest in the upward struggles of their people in the past and a determination to do their part toward the progress of their race in the future. Always seek to create a spirit of love and brotherhood in the minds of the children toward the white people, and in telling them the history of the Indians dwell on those things which have showed nobility of character on the part of either race in their dealings with the other.

Study the arts and industries of the Indians in the past.

Compare the Indian life of the past with its present and what it should and will be in the future; the houses the old Indians built; their food, occupations, and manner of living. Tell them that their history will be what they make it, and they should feel the responsibility for making it bright. Dwell upon agriculture, its history, and its importance to the Indian. Discuss the various products that can be raised and the best crops to be raised.

Give attention to the other industries of the old Indians, encouraging the discontinuance of those which are unprofitable and the preservation of the practice of those which are valuable, such as basketry, pottery, blanketry, etc.

Have the children bring baskets to school and make some themselves, all of which place on exhibition, and encourage the pupils to become as skillful as possible. Native weaves and the natural Indian dyes are the most valuable. Follow the same plan with respect to bead work and pottery.

Take up the subject of the buffalo and thence lead up to cattle raising and dairying. Find out how cattle figured in the history of the old Indians and how it will figure in the lives of the Indians of the future. Study cattle raising, the different breeds and those best suited to the locality, their feed, different grasses and grain raised for feed; their care, housing, pasturage; how profitable, either for beef of dairy purposes; the available markets, etc.

Take up in a like manner the other industries, such as the raising of hogs and poultry.

Irrigation will also be a valuable subject for study in many localities where it is necessary for farming.

Then give instruction in the history of the United States. It is not desired that American history be studied with much detail, but rather a general view of it given the pupils. They should know enough about it to be good, patriotic citizens, but valuable time should not be used in learning minor details. They should learn a few important dates, such as that of the discovery of America, settlement of Virginia, Declaration of Independence, etc.

Describe historical events, as the discovery of America and the landing of the Pilgrims.

The important events in our history, such as the great wars, should be given attention, but not in detail. Show the causes of the various wars, what were their principal results, and who were the great actors in them. The names of our greatest men, such as Washington, Franklin, and Lincoln, should also be learned and something about the character and work of each.

Employ public anniversaries and the birthdays of great men, like Lincoln, Washington, and Longfellow, to give historical information-points of general interest, not minute details.

Adapt also stories appropriate to Thanksgiving, Christmas, New Year's Day, Arbor Day, etc.

Enlarge upon national holidays; history of our flag; patriotism; loyalty to a cause, one's institution, one's country.

Teach the general character of the Government of the United States and how it is conducted. Explain its relations with the Indians.

Give lessons in State and local government; how public officers are chosen; the principle of self-government. Explain the three branches of government, executive, legislative, and judicial. Explain in a simple way the workings of a court.

The central thought is preparation for citizenship.

Correlate history and language, requiring all stories to be retold in good English,

Housekeeping

The art of housekeeping as learned in the home under the mother's eye is what we want to teach our Indian girls, assuring them that because our grandmothers did things in a certain way is no reason why we should do the same. The good housekeeper is the arbiter of the health of the occupants of the home, and special stress must be laid upon the hygienic and sanitary laws. Let all the sunshine possible into the homes and lives of the family.

Attention must be given to the food eaten, the water used, and the air surrounding the home, to the furniture of the house, and to the manners and morals of the members of the family. Unselfishness, consideration for others, and a spirit of helpfulness, together with a sense of right and wrong, constitute good habits and manners of the individual members of the household. "A happy, healthful home is the foundation upon which the welfare of the family and the prosperity of the nation rest," and a systematic knowledge of things relating to the home is a lesson all girls should learn.

Every girl should be taught to make yeast, to make and bake all kinds of bread, to cook cereals, meats, vegetables (boiling and steaming), soups, plain pastry, cookies, cake, to dress and cook poultry, to prepare eggs in a number of palatable ways, to prepare beverages, to do simple invalid cooking, warmed-over dishes, and to utilize unconsumed food. Attention must be given to the hygienic conditions of the kitchen and surroundings, exercising great care that refuse be placed where it can not sink into the drinking water.

Drinking water should never stand uncovered. The value of pure water can not be too strongly impressed, for, as a well-known writer has said, "this fluid, which infuses new life into mankind, is likewise the chief vehicle by which disease and death enter the body."

Since "the destiny of the nation depends upon its food," it is important that we show these Indian children that their first duty is to help build up a strong physical organism. Nothing so weakens the brain as lack of nutrition.

Pupils must be taught to cut, fit, and make all kinds of wearing apparel and all articles needed for the household, and to be resourceful, using very scrap in some way, throwing away nothing. Economy in housekeeping is an all-important lesson.

Teach girls to care for the sick, to dress wounds, put on bandages, and simple appliances for the relief of pain, thus fitting them for the emergencies that come to every home.

The importance of teaching the laundry work in a systematic way is very great. Pupils must be taught to make good soap. Impress the importance of mending clothes before washing, and to wash, starch, and iron all kinds of wearing apparel and household linen. Teach sweeping, dusting, care of lamps, washing windows, care of woodwork, care of kitchen, of floors, of cellar, and the disposal of household refuse.

Study the bent of each girl, giving each the help in special directions that she needs most.

Have the girls take turns in the management and care of the house, the sweeping, scrubbing, and dusting; the care of beds, filling up all cracks and holes with putty, that vermin may have no place in which to breed; the care of bedding, seeing that it is kept clean and properly aired, and that beds are neatly made.

Show the importance of keeping sleeping rooms well aired during the day, and that no food should ever be kept in a room where people sleep.

The dignity of labor should be impressed upon the mind of the Indian student, and the virtue of economy should be emphasized. Children should be taught to put to the very best use what is so generously supplied by the Government. If there is time for nothing else, housekeeping must be taught.

The materials supplied by the school for the pupils must be used, and in a variety of ways, and the pupils must be taught cooking as done for a small family. This work may be placed under the immediate direction of the cook, and every day one girl should prepare an entire meal for one table in the dining room.

Teach pupils the bad results of running bills at shops. Cash payments should always be made, and the income of the family so divided that the housekeeper will set aside a certain portion for household expenses and live with that amount.

Reverses and illness come to the best regulated families, and it is wisdom to have simple, well-cooked food, simplicity in dress and living, and a bank account to resort to in time of need.

Laundry

The training in doing laundry work begins the first year the child enters school. This highly necessary lesson cannot be commenced too early in life, and the first year in school it will be presented in such an attractive manner that the child will enjoy assisting in the work, and be given one of the most important lessons that must be learned. It is not expected that children will appreciate the importance of well bleached linen and fault-lessly smooth ironing, but it is intended that from the start they shall be trained in doing laundry work systematically and see the necessity for hygienic living.

With the youngest children the teacher must have a proper place and receptacle for all soiled linen used in the doll's house, never putting any away damp, least it mildew. On wash day the clothes must be properly sorted, washed, and dried out of doors if possible; if not they may be hung on lines strung across the window. On ironing day they are ironed, then mended, and when thoroughly dry put a way, neatly folded.

Each pupil should have a laundry bag and be responsible for personal apparel. This fosters responsibility and will tend to make children take better care of their clothing. The matron must see that every garment is plainly marked with the name of the owner, thus avoiding confusion and enabling garments to be located. Clothing that is common property is rarely appreciated as personal belongings are. This is a lesson the Indian child needs to learn.

Small children can assist in the laundry, staying an hour at first and gradually increasing the time as the child develops physically. Have small irons for the smaller children to use and put them on the simplest garments, towels, etc.

It is always wise to have at least one girl on the laundry detail at all times who is thoroughly familiar with the work and in whose care the smaller pupils may be placed, that the experienced pupil may assist the little ones just learning, helping them with the difficult parts, and showing them how whenever they need advice and assistance. In this way the laundress will have a trained class of helpers each year.

In laundries where the work is heavy and must be done by machinery, the laundress must have a few tubs and teach pupils how to wash on boards. This must be taught every pupil. When pupils return to their homes, they will have few facilities for doing laundry work, and at school they must be taught to do the work with the most limited outfit.

So much of the health and comfort of life depends upon the cleansing of clothing and linen need in the family that the subject can not be studied too carefully.

The laundry must be supplied with oilcloth aprons that pupils may not get their clothing wet when washing at tubs. Overshoes should be worn by pupils when floors are wet or when they have to walk on damp ground. Pupils must not be allowed to go out to hang up or bring in clothes when overheated, and they should have a jacket or cape to protect the lungs, and some covering for the head in bad weather. Good health is one of man's greatest blessings and must be guarded intelligently.

The laundress and her assistants will be expected to do all the laundry work of the school, including wearing apparel for boys and girls, table and bed linen, curtains, towels, and everything that is needed for the comfort and well being of the pupils.

All body linen should be changed at least once a week and individual towels and handkerchiefs must be supplied pupils. Bureaus and tables should be supplied with neat covers which pupils should take pride in keeping well laundered. It is well to wash comforts and blankets at least once a year. Dresses and aprons should be starched since they keep clean much longer.

Pupils must be taught in the laundry to use fires economically, to sort and wash white and colored clothes; the different ways of washing, rinsing, wringing, bluing, and starching clothes; the making of soap and starch, also their use; using lye; drying clothes out of doors and in the house; sprinkling and ironing clothes; care of laundry, tubs, buckets, utensils, machinery, and irons. The object is to teach all pupils to be able to do family washing expeditiously and thoroughly.

The school laundry is maintained not only to keep the clothing used at the school in proper condition, but to train the pupils in habits of cleanliness and civilized ways of living and for hygienic reasons. Pupils must be taught the work in a systematic way and the training must be so thorough that pupils will see and feel the reasons for washing articles clean and making them look as attractive as possible. They must be shown the inadvisability of keeping soiled clothing in a sleeping room and in sorting clothes properly, washing white and colored pieces separately. They must be taught to use plenty of soap, to rub soiled things on a board (using a scrubbing brush on heavy-soiled garments), rinsing properly and drying in the open, air, and finally ironing smoothly.

Music

Froebel believed that music greatly assisted the development of all the powers of the child; that it awakens the moral life, elevates the spiritual tone, and gives relief to physical weariness; therefore in the kindergarten the child is given songs and mother plays which are full of music.

Pure tone must be sought. This will be aided by using a pleasant tone in speaking; therefore cultivate it in all recitations and conversations.

The position of the body and throat while singing should contribute to the full expansion of the lungs; not only must the mouth be open nearly as wide as nature will allow, but the throat also must be open.

In the lowest grades the children may be given a few simple rote songs illustrating the lesson to be impressed. Have them sing in a natural soft tone, never permitting nasal tones.

A few exercises in breathing should be given before singing, and see that all children assume a proper position while singing.

Patriotic songs must be taught and the children told something of the life of the author and the reasons for writing the songs given.

Every evening at the study hour, or what should be termed the recreation hour, the pupils may be given fifteen minutes drill on sight reading from the chart and blackboard, the scales, tonic drill, and part singing.

It is not the desire of the Department to give advanced instructions in music, but it is intended to be taught more as a recreation, whose uplifting influence will be felt in the home.

Source: U.S. Commissioner of Indian Affairs. Report of the Superintendent of Indian Schools, 1901.

WHITE HOUSE CONFERENCE
ON INDIAN EDUCATION

A congressional report issued in November 1969 entitled "Indian Education: A National Tragedy—A National Challenge" made many recommendations for improvement of education for Native Americans in the United States, including the need for a White House conference. That report concluded that the failure of national educational policies and practices for Native Americans lay in the exclusion of American Indians from the planning process, and believed that a White House conference would reverse this trend. Senator DeConcini (Arizona) introduced Senate Bill 1645 in August 1987, the Indian Education Amendments Act. The hearings on this bill led to the idea of the White House Conference, which did live up to its expectations. Each state held a pre-conference, which involved Native American educators, and forwarded their findings and recommendations to the White House Conference. The delegates to the White House Conference were primarily Native American educators, and the results of that conference were a series of resolutions that can be found in the final report of the White House Conference on Indian Education. The excerpt below was taken from that document's Executive Summary.

Executive Summary Analysis

Goals of Analysis

The goals of the Conference were categorized as education oriented. However the affected constituency and delegates did not confine their vision to the "traditional" construct of the definition of education.

Indian families and communities are very aware that the needs of their children are interwoven into all aspects of their lifes [*sic*]. American Indian and Alaska Native communities have strong foundation of spiritual beliefs and philosophies most of which encompass the circular nature of life that upholds the interconnection between all beings and things. It was this outlook that provided the reenforcement to the White House Conference on Indian Education to address the educational needs in a holistic manner.

The task for collecting concerns which impacted the educational services of Indian communities, were drawn from a wide array of sources. It was the responsibility of the Task Force to attempt to portray these issues and concerns for the delegate's consideration in the most inter-related form possible.

The Task Force designed a matrix which appeared to embody the Indian community's identified issues of concern (see the full report). This circular matrix represented the all-encompassing nature of both issues and possible solutions. This "dream catcher's" universe of needs and opportunities' is symbolic of the circumstances confronting Indian community. On one hand, the barriers and specific elements which comprise the present reality must be "caught" and addressed, but the goals and aspirations must also be sought and fostered.

This analysis will depict the issues by these goals and aspirations, as well as the means or mechanism proposed by the Delegates to resolve or eliminate barriers. The commonalities of concerns and recommendations, from topic area to topic area, will be identified for policy purposes. When differences in policy goals are proposed, for similar or overlapping issues and recommendations, these will also be summarized. This summary will portray these overlapping recommendations juxtaposed against those policies or issues they address to differentiate the instigating cause or intended outcome; such as local community control over actions which may be defined as a new effort and entity, or identified as tribally-controlled.

The resultant blue print for action will also convey future policy issues and implications. The many levels of involvement and action that are required to implement these recommendations will require comprehensive participation by all affected parties. When and how, such endeavors, from local Indian communities to national policy makers, should be undertaken are questions that this report should provoke.

Parameters of the Conference and Issues

The Conference was designed to be a "working" conference to develop long-term and short-term strategies from recommendations adopted by the Delegates. The 30 state and regional pre-conference activities, produced numerous recommendations for consideration by the Conference Delegates. The Delegates were mailed materials prior to the Conference which contained specific instructions to assist Delegates in their review and preparation. However, the range of issues and the number of issues, as well as other constraints, combined to place limitations on both the selection of issues chosen and the amount of specificity available for guidance.

The same limitations that existed for review of Pre-Conference recommendations also affected the consideration of new issues raised during the Conference. There were some issues raised on the final day of the Conference that were additional issues of concern, but only four resolutions capturing these concerns were eventually adopted. Another factor was the inherent assumption that many of the Delegates had with respect to key principles underlying Federal-Indian issues. One key principle was that of respective powers and responsibilities of tribal, State and Federal governments. Further, it was expected that how these governments inter-related with one another, and their affiliate entities, was also understood, particularly in relationship to the need for change or action.

Another assumption was the level of clarity expressed in the many resolutions and plans of action in the area of statutory and administrative authority targeted for change or action. Some topic areas were very precise on what legislation should be amended and how, or what a legislative amendment ought to accomplish. Some topic areas felt that the Executive Branch was the place to impact, through recommendations for development and adoption of Executive Orders. Other topic areas proposed that much more explicit action take place with regards to programs and issues.

Such programs or issues were often identified solely by acronym or original public law citation.

These assumptions require a prior understanding of tribes and their relationship with the United States, to fully appreciate the Conference Delegates' concerns and their proposed solutions.

The Federal-Indian relationship is not one well understood by the general society. For many individuals, their sole exposure to "Indians" has been provided through movies and the print media from a non-Indian view and, usually, in the absence of accurate historical background. This deficiency in society's learning environment is at the root of some of the recommendations adopted by the Conference Delegates. A brief explanation is provided below to aid in understanding the Federal-Indian relationship. The Federal government has a government-to-government, political relationship with tribes that is rooted in the Constitution and further strengthened by congressionally-ratified treaties, Executive Orders, case law, and specific and general statutes to assist American Indian and Alaska Native communities and individuals. This relationship even pre-dates the Declaration of Independence, when the colonial powers entered into formal agreements with tribes to exchange lands for peace, goods, and other purposes.

When the United States declared its independence and, eventually, adopted its constitution, there were three key clauses incorporated into this charter for the protection and benefit of tribes and their people. This provision, under Article I, Section 8, Clause 3 stated that only the United States (and not States) had the power to regulate and permit commerce with tribes. Article II, section 2, clause 2 grants Congress plenary power to regulate commerce with Indian tribes, as it does with foreign nations and the States. Section 14, Amendment XIV of the Constitution also exempts tribes from taxation. Subsequently, the courts, based on these authorities, recognized that tribes, as dependent nations, were beneficiaries of a trust responsibility on the part of the United States.

These principles of Federal-Indian law have been tested over the past two centuries. Yet, for the most part, the rights of tribes as sovereign nations whose relationship is with the United States first, and not those States or territories in which they reside, have been upheld.

As this relationship has been strengthened through successive laws and Executive Orders, and as tribes have continued their efforts to determine their own future, the nature of the relationship has also evolved. Where once Federal agencies decided what was appropriate and beneficial to tribes without tribal input, now there is recognition that tribal self-determination is one elemental aspect of their sovereignty. It is the principle of sovereignty and self-determination which underlies many of the issues raised and addressed by the delegates during the Conference. Each tribe has variations in its performance of its responsibilities to their people; based, in part, on the issue or region in which they are located. What may be true for one tribe, for regulating the environment, health and other programs, may not be accurate for other tribes. The reasons for this variation among tribal groups are many and complex. That they exist and create additional barriers, and sometimes opportunities, is a critical element in the development of the many adopted strategies by the Conference Delegates to improve Indian education.

Additionally, during the past fifty years, as Indian people relocated "off-reservation", either under Federal actions and policies or for their own purposes, there has grown a community of Indian people outside the traditional bounds of "Indian lands". These segments of the population, often identified as rural or urban Indians, are now identified more as members of their home communities rather than as displaced and unaffiliated individuals. The location of these rural and urban Indian people has placed special needs and demands for services to aid their growth and well-being.

The complexity of the Federal-Tribal relationship needs to be considered when reviewing the adopted resolutions and plans of action. This complexity and the inter-dependency between American Indian and Alaska Native people requires that careful planning and action be undertaken to implement strategies for improvements.

This analysis will identify concerns which require a balancing of competing needs and a means for transition from existing efforts to new activities. The balancing and transition issues, where not addressed by the Delegates in their resolution and plans of action, will especially require a general understanding of the relationships and roles between the United State[s] and American Indian / Alaska Native communities and people.

Analysis

The Conference Delegates endorsed several major goals, which were designed to achieve improved student outcomes and services. The resolutions were designed to emphasize accountability to improved standards, including culturally appropriate ones. However, the predominant underlying principle was the premise that the Federal-Tribal relationship entailed specific duties and responsibilities on the part of the United States, unlike any other Federal-State-Local governmental relationship.

The consistent call by the delegates for the United States to recognize and reaffirm the Federal-Tribal relationship indicates the serious concerns that exist over whether Federal policy makers fully appreciate and understand how their actions affect this relationship. This repeated call expressed a desire to require departments and agencies to uphold this principle in daily operations and reflects a desire to expand and strengthen tribal participation on several fronts.

A strengthened U.S. policy is also expected to provide the dictates necessary to accomplish the more practical activities in realizing equitable access to all relevant resources to produce the desired achievements. There is a valid concern expressed that all Federal agencies make an equal effort to assist tribes and Indian communities. Without a concerted outreach effort there will be a continued lack of tribal participation and access to available resources. The absence of participation and access to opportunities can create limited outcomes which will diminished [*sic*] capabilities for elevating the quality of life for Indian people.

One major theme that was articulated was the premise that tribal control and leadership in education was critical in the strengthening of services. Local control and determination of needs is a demand and goal of all segments of society. Indian country is not different in this respect, but there is additional weight behind this demand given the inability of society to accurately perceive the cultural aspects integral to the values and goals of Indian communities.

Both local control and determination of needs must be viewed in conjunction with another major theme of the inclusion, at every educational level, of appropriate cultural values, language, beliefs, accurate histories, and other expressions. Indian and Alaska Native life is built on the foundation of their tribal beliefs and identity. Yet, obtaining respect for, and fostering such components in an "traditional" education system, have not been very successful. A number of recommendations adopted addressed stronger tribal control over the incorporation of cultural facets in the reform and restructuring of these "traditional/formal" educational systems.

The Delegates did not overlook the need to instill or enhance governmental partnerships among affected entities, tribes, States, Federal, and other bodies. This major theme was an indication of the Indian community's need to interact more with other entities, as well as become involved in the larger issues confronting all communities.

This comprehensive approach should be viewed as an integral aspect of all the key principles and themes. In particular, when undertaking efforts to identify the scope of educational needs in Indian communities, there are concerns that education needs encompass all related issues and services for all ages and members of the community. Related issues and services were not so broadly interpreted that it could become a Herculean task. The parameters placed on education and related issues or services appeared to be whether there were direct correlation between a service and improved student outcomes, such areas as substance abuse prevention, family violence prevention, and career guidance.

The other key indicator in defining relevance was the correlation between the benefits derived by Indian communities and improved student outcomes. Two examples include the proposed requirement that economic enterprises provide employment in a manner planned by the tribe to coincide with graduating scholarship recipients, and requiring "pay back obligations" by students upon graduation for their scholarship assistance.

There are certain aspects that were not fully addressed or resolved by the Conference Delegates. The unresolved issues did not occur by premeditation or an unwillingness to tackle these issues.

The Delegates were required to work within the various topic areas in which they participated, plus review and approve those resolutions in the final day of the Conference from other topic groups. Consequently, the Delegates were simply unable to fully reflect on the complete picture presented by their combined efforts. The Delegates began an effort to address and accurately present a comprehensive overview of education and related needs. These actions asserted that such needs should be locally-determined since the affected Indian people and communities would be most able to recognize and ascertain these needs. While this is an important point, the ability to integrate this activity with the recommendation requiring that funds and services be provided on an equitable basis, becomes problematic.

The assumption to the first resolution is that there are, or will be, clearly understood and accepted criteria for determining true needs in all areas. The second recommendation's assumption is that the funds will be provided in sufficient amounts to ensure equitability, to provide "comparable" services in obtaining similar goals, such as eliminating illiteracy, substance abuse, and dropout rates.

To begin an administrative process for developing criteria for determining the "scope of need" requires several basic components. First, the data on eligible service population and present level of services available must be current. Second, a clearly defined goal of what is to be achieved through services to be provided must be understood and acceptable to the beneficiary population. Third, how growth will be achieved from the present status to the desired goals must be developed, approved and implemented. Each of these components will require an investment in manpower, resources, and time. When to apply this strategy to the targeted education or related program services must also be determined.

When the definition of need was raised, it was through the provision of services to "American Indian/Alaska Native" people. Yet, many available services are dependent on a variety of factors. Eligibility for services is not consistent from program to program, and agency to agency. One topic group addressed the abolition of the income eligibility requirement for the Head Start Program.

Another topic group recommended that eligibility for "Indian education services" should be in keeping with the respective tribal definitions and requirements for member enrollment. When tribes, tribal or Indian organizations provide services for their populations, a uniform definition for eligibility would eliminate multiple program requirements that must be fulfilled.

Overall, transitioning services into a means of accomplishing the identified education goals is not a process that can be precisely detailed. However, there are ground rules that should be considered on the difficulties confronting such transition. These ground rules include: where tribal input is needed; estimated time frames to accomplish identified tasks, level of risk involved and disclosure of advantages and disadvantages nationally and locally.

Recommendations and plans of action are not specific with respect to priority setting, other than needs and solutions should be tribally and locally determined. In order to have an effective process to implement the many education goals and tasks identified by the Conference Delegates, a means of ensuring fairness in priority setting and equitable allocation of resources must be planned and provided. For example, if certain actions throughout the country are expected to occur concurrently, assistance to Indian communities must follow common national criteria, yet be locally relevant. Specifically, pre-school screening for exceptional and challenged Indian children has been recommended to be joined with efforts to expand early childhood services. This activity will require cooperative efforts in a multi-disciplinary and multi-agency manner.

Potential Issues of Immediacy

There were common issues that Delegates expressed throughout the resolutions and plans of action. These issues were focused on providing resources to ensure a higher quality of standards and services.

Many recommendations have the potential for immediate implementation, utilizing existing authorities of the relevant agencies. There are recommendations which clearly require new authority, and a close scrutiny of agencys' present authorities could determine which issues can be promoted absent such new authority. In some instances, new authority would be useful in preventing any action to transfer funds from one program into a new program diminishing available resources in the drained program.

Conclusion

The resolutions and plans of action adopted by the Conference Delegates are far reaching and, often, interdependent. It is a tremendous accolade to the Delegates that the Conference's work products are so comprehensive and thoughtful.

It will be this same spirit and commitment which will be required to undertake the actions needed to achieve these identified goals and tasks.

The issues that the Delegates addressed can be viewed as a map for the future of Indian education and other related needs. This future is perceived to be inclusive of benefits to both Indian and non- Indian people and communities.

These resolutions and plans of action require each person, community, and institution, to evaluate themselves for their strengths and capabilities. By contributing to each other to achieve better learning environments and student outcomes, the rewards increase exponentially throughout all spectrums of our society.

Source: White House Conference on Indian Education. The Final Report of the White House Conference on Indian Education: Executive Summary Analysis, May 22, 1992. Washington, DC: White House Conference on Indian Education, 1992.

GERTRUDE GOLDEN, *RED MOON CALLED ME* [EXCERPT AND TWO LETTERS]

Golden was one of many single white women who made up nearly half of the teachers in the Bureau of Indian Affairs. She became a teacher at age 15, and accepted her first BIA teaching position at a boarding school in Oregon in 1901, when she was 27 years old. She went on to teach in many on- and off-reservation boarding schools until she retired from the BIA in 1918. In 1954, her memoir of her teaching career was published. In it, she included letters written by some of her students in English. These help to give a voice to the many Native American students who attended boarding school. She also candidly tells the story of a student who returned to the reservation from Carlisle boarding school, and how his boarding school education impeded his success on the reservation, rather than enhanced it. This was a common criticism of Native American boarding school education, also voiced by Zitkala-Sa and Luther Standing Bear. Though not a universal result for all boarding school students, the one-size-fits-all nature of the boarding school curriculum could and did produce some dysfunctional graduates.

Red Moon Called Me

Miguel

MIGUEL was a strong-faced, intelligent old Indian who had been an orderly to an officer in the days when Fort Yuma was occupied by United States troops. Through this association he had learned some English and had become familiar with a good many of the white man's ways. Miguel lived with his wife in a slightly better hogan than that of his neighbors on the reservation near the school. His wife kept this home as clean as a hut with a mud could be kept. Under the tutelage of the Sisters she had learned to sew, embroider and make lace, and through these accomplishments she was able to add somewhat to the meager family income.

This couple had three fine-looking, intelligent sons, the eldest two of whom were at Carlisle in the government school. The other, a lad of seventeen, had just completed a course at Fort Yuma and was planning to join his brothers at Carlisle for further education and training in some trade.

The evening Ambrose left for Carlisle several of his schoolmates, we teachers and his father were there to see him off. His mother had bidden him farewell at home, not feeling equal to the effort of restraining her grief at parting with this youngest son in the presence of so many staring white people.

While waiting for the train, Ambrose, dapper in his clothes such as any white boy might have worn on such an occasion, talked and joked with his schoolmates and teachers, seemingly unmindful of his father who, with bent head, paced up and down the platform awaiting the parting moment. What a contrast with his son! He was barefoot, with his heavy, iron-gray hair off square at the shoulders and tied about the forehead with a bright-hued handkerchief, gay cotton shirt open at the neck and cotton trousers.

When at last the train pulled in, Ambrose approached his father and gave him his hand in farewell. It was to be a five-year parting from Miguel's only remaining son. They shed no tears. The old man put a hand on his son's shoulder and said something in their own language. Then the train whistled. Amid a chorus of good-bys from his schoolmates, Ambrose bounded up the steps and was soon waving a last farewell from a rapidly moving window.

Without a word to anyone, old Miguel turned away, fearing we might see the sorrow he was determined to hide, and took his lone way into the darkness, across the railroad bridge to his hogan where the companion of this new loneliness awaited him.

They had now given up and sent away their third and last son to be educated by their traditional enemies and conquerors—to be educated according to the standards of the whites which were, in most particulars, opposite to those inherited from their Yuma ancestors. This five-year separation from their sons would separate them, not for that stated period only, but forever, through a complete change in thinking, in ideals and in outlook.

A few months later the meaning of this separation was impressed upon me more strongly than ever before. Miguel's eldest son, having finished at Carlisle and graduated as a carpenter, came home after six years' absence. He was a good-looking, clean, healthy youth of twenty-four or five, well dressed in the latest mode.

At Carlisle there was employed what was called the outing-system which provided that the pupils should be placed out among townspeople or farmers of the state, there to work for their board and clothes while they attended public school in the neighborhood. They were permitted to go into families only where they would be surrounded by the best influences and receive the best of treatment. So young Miguel had for six years been living either at the Carlisle Boarding School or with well-to-do Christian families. In these places he had enjoyed modern conveniences along with a few luxuries, perhaps, and had been so accustomed to them that they had become prime necessities in his life. The old couple welcomed the son who had been so long away from them with eager arms and hopeful hearts, thinking, no doubt, that he would be a prop in their old age and comfort them for the loss of Ambrose, recently gone. But alas! They had sent an Indian to Carlisle, and he had returned a white man. He could no longer sleep on a mud floor rolled up in a blanket. He must have a clean bed, so he came up to the school to spend the nights. He could no longer sit on a mud floor around a campfire and eat mesquite beans and tortillas; he must have well-cooked white man's food, served on a table with clean dishes and linen. So he ate most of his meals at the school or in restaurants in the town.

Young Miguel could find little carpenter work in Yuma where most of the houses were adobe and where little building of any sort was going on; so, after hanging around the reservation for a month, living mostly at the school, he again bade farewell to his parents and started for Los Angeles to try to find work at his trade among prejudiced and unsympathetic strangers. It was then, without a doubt, that old Miguel and his wife fully realized that their sons were separated from them forever.

Short-sighted people have a great deal to say in condemnation of the "return to the blanket" of the educated Indians, little realizing the hardships and disillusionment which await these youths upon leaving their boarding schools. They are trained for a job which cannot be found. They face competition with the whites as well as race prejudice wherever they go. Further, there is the powerful influence of parents and reservation friends who taunt the returning student with charges that he is aping the dress, manners and customs of his white conquerors.

Nor do these narrow-minded critics realize the great sacrifice of the parents who love their children just as white parents do, yet give them up to be trained to disregard age-old traditions of the Indian and follow the "White Man's Road." It is hard for the childlike native mind to look ahead for generations and be able to realize the ultimate' benefits of education to their race. The transition period from a primitive way of living to an age of enlightenment is hard on all concerned. (pp.86–88)

[. . .]

First Day at School

Chilocco, Okla., May, 1909

My first teacher, her name was Miss Thomas. When I first went to school in [*sic*] was Sunday at dinner time. First they cut off my long hair and then dressed me in school clothes. At the table I could not eat hard bread and hard meat and strong coffee.

When I first went to school it was strange to hear them talk English and write, but I know how to read and write some. My father and mother teach me ABC's and to read primer and chart. It wasn't very strange to me and it wasn't hard to me and I wasn't ever lonesome or homesick.

My first disciplinarian was Mr. Bothwell, and the first place I had to work was in the carpenter shop. When I first went sleep I was kind scared, but my brother was in school and he sleep with me.

Before I came to school, I was very anxious to come so I could learn. My mother and father used to tell me not to swear and not to run away. And I never know how to run away. I never did run away in my life, and *that's the Gospel truth.*

By Willie Blackbeard

Chilocco, Okla., May, 1909

My folks tole me I must go to school but I don't like to go; they always sayin that to me, bye and bye I go to school. So my father took me to the school. When my father went away, I was not feelin good. I didn't talk to anyone, because I don't know these children at school. Some of them is mean to me sometime, too, and make me cry. By and by I got a friend, and now I am happy with him.

The teacher was trying to talk to me. I didn't say a thing because I don't understand them what they mean. In the school was very hard lesson for me. When my teacher try to make me read, I won't do it, and so she sometime whip me, trying to make me read. I was scared, and when we have vacation I went home and tell my folks all about how I was doin in school.

By Charlie Tallbear

Source: Golden, Gertrude. *Red Moon Called Me.* San Antonio: Naylor, 1954.

RICHARD HENRY PRATT'S LETTER TO THADDEUS POUND OF THE HOUSE OF REPRESENTATIVES

This copy of Pratt's letter to Thaddeus Pound of the House of Representatives explains in his own words the successes of the new boarding school he established at Carlisle, Pennsylvania, for Native American children. Pratt's belief that the American Indian students were equal to the Anglo-American students in terms of intellect and ability fueled his zeal to educate them to take their place in society alongside their Anglo brothers and sisters. Unfortunately, he viewed their own indigenous education, culture, background, and language as nothing more than a barrier to their success in American society, and actively attempted to eradicate cultural indicators in his school. His model of education and cultural genocide was followed by all succeeding boarding schools established and funded by the government.

Indian Industrial School,
Carlisle Barracks,
January 13, 1881.

Hon. Thaddeus C. Pound,
U. S. House of Representatives,
Washington, D.C.

Dear Governor:

I wish you could get a delegation of the Indian Committees of Congress to come up and see our school before the session closes.

It seems to me that the educational question with the Indians just now is the vital point. Whether the Bill you proposed in the House and which has been so favorably reported upon twice by the Indian Committee, is best or not of course is for you to determine. It seems to me there can be no wiser use of the abandoned military posts and barracks than this and if the movement, which has been urged by the War Department for several years past to concentrate the army into posts of large command for purposes of economy, should be brought about, many more posts would be available for this purpose, in very many of which all needs for shelter and school purposes are satisfactory, without material additional expense and many of them have an abundance of arable land where agriculture can be taught. The use of these posts for a few years longer, before being sold, as is customary, would be no detriment to the government because the lands and property would be increased value all the time.

There is no doubt but that a well directed effort for the education and training of all Indian youth of suitable age can be made successful and certainly nothing will tend more to save us from a large pauper and vagabond population. I know that Indian children of nomadic parents, properly trained, can be made self-supporting men and women. They can learn to speak the English language, they can take on a fair education, and be trained industrially in civilized pursuits, they can be made self-supporting and industrious, and I think these facts will be apparent to the members of Congress who may come to look at our work here.

The weakness of this effort and all other efforts to help the Indian up, is the leaving of such a large "pull down" element unhelped. By the treaties we have now in force with the Sioux; Cheyennes, Arapahoes, Kiowas, Comanches, Pawnees, Navajoes, Utes, Shoshones, Bannocks and some other tribes, they have a full and complete claim upon the government for educational privileges for *all* their children. If in the future we find our country burdened and troubled with these people it will be in a great measure due to our failure in carrying out our treaty stipulations with them in this regard. We have promised to give to all the children school privileges and they are now ready to receive them. Delays dishearten and discourage them.

It is pressed upon me here continually that it would not be a difficult task to gather into school training all the children of these tribes. Partial effort invites partial failure. All educational work for the Indians is good; I believe that the system of removing them from their tribes and placing them under continuous training in the midst of civilization is far better than any other method. In an Indian school at an Agency the civilizing influences are limited to the instructors with perhaps a few examples of agency employees, with a tremendous pull against what they may do in the persons of the fathers and mothers and all the members of the tribe. In fact, such an effort might properly be called theoretical, while here, or removed from their tribes and placed in the midst of civilization, the teaching is all practical, all the surroundings help. The industrious farmer and mechanic is in sight daily. The evidence that man must obtain his living by the sweat of his brow is constantly before the children and it becomes an easy matter for them to join with the sentiment of the community in that direction. We had difficulty at first to get our boys and girls to work but now I am frequently asked by the students to be permitted to work more than our school regulations require. Boys esteemed too young to be put at trades frequent the shops, witness the productions of the older ones in harness making, tin ware, boots and shoes, clothing, blacksmith and wagon making, and they ask to be permitted to learn a trade. The few put out on farms during vacation are anxious to go back. One boy, who for the sake of health, I permitted to remain with a farmer over his time, has formed such a liking for farm work that he begs to be allowed to remain through the winter. The farmer finds him particularly useful in caring for the stock and doing the chores with his own boys, so that he is glad to have him remain. He goes to school with the farmer's children and thus being isolated he learns English rapidly. His health has improved very much. A girl that I had allowed to remain with a farmer for some time formed such an attachment for the place that she calls it home and cries to go back to learn to milk cows and bake pies and cakes. My purpose is during the coming summer vacation to plant out with the good farmers of this valley all the boys and girls whom we cannot use in the shops and upon our farm. I am sure that if we could bring to bear such training as this upon all our Indian children for only three years, that savagery among the Indians in this country would be at an end. This bringing their children east among the whites is to many of them now, and would be to all in time, an open door by which they can migrate into civilization. I can see by their correspondence and by what the parents say to me when visiting here that they appreciate most highly this privilege and desire to make use of it. The Cheyenne and Arapahoe chiefs when here, after understanding what I intended to do in the way of putting children out, all asked that their children be put out in this way. They want their children to see just how the white man lives. White Eagle, the Ponca chief who was here a few days ago, speaking for all the chiefs who were with him, approved in the strongest terms all that he saw. He said among other things that for a very long time it seemed as though the Great Spirit had forgotten all about the Indians but just now when he saw what privileges their children had, how fast they were learning in the school and how well they worked in the shops, he believed the Great Spirit was remembering the Indians and was now going to help them. Having all the affection of the most loving father for his boy, both of them crying and embracing each other warmly at parting, he as well as the other chiefs cheerfully left their children and said they would send more if I would take them.

This effort is to these far-seeing leaders among the Indians evidence that they are to be permitted to become like the whites, that their declarations that they "want to travel upon the white man's road" are at last accepted. That in fact there is a hope that they may become citizens of this country and as such have the rights, privileges and protection granted to other citizens and that before this grave responsibility is thrust upon them they are to be in some measure provided and prepared for it by education and training in just exactly the same way that the white man is prepared for the same status; that is, by education and training their, and our youth together.

I invite your attention to the report of the Honorable Commissioner of Indian Affairs for 1880, pages VII and VIII where our work is mentioned by the Commissioner and to what is said upon education by the several Agents on pages 26, 45, 48, 59, 69, 75, 84, 117 and 134. These testimonies from the Agents of the tribes whose children are represented here ought to have great weight.

This system, which is so very new and necessarily imperfect, can be made to exert an influence upon the civilization of the Indians greater, to my mind, than it is possible to effect with the same expenditure in any other direction.

By every means that I have been able to bring to bear I have invited inspection and criticism and if you concur with me in the wisdom of a Congressional visit I would specially desire that those in Congress who are prejudiced and unbelievers should be of the party. I believe that a visit might be arranged so that by leaving Washington early you could spend four or five hours with us and return the same night. Could this be brought about?

> Very respectfully yours,
> R. H. Pratt,
> Lieut.

Source: Pratt, Richard Henry. *Battlefield and Classroom: Four Decades with the American Indian, 1867–1904.* New Haven: Yale University Press, 1964.

███████████

ZITKALA-SA, "THE CUTTING OF MY LONG HAIR"

Zitkala-Sa, born Gertrude Simmons on the Pine Ridge reservation, traveled east to Indiana to attend a Quaker missionary school at age eight. She went on to attend Earlham College and to teach at Carlisle Indian School. Later, she became a writer and an activist for Native American rights, founding the National Council for American Indians in 1926.

Although she attended a missionary boarding school and not a government boarding school, her description of her initial days at the boarding school, including her haircut and issuance of new clothing, were quite typical of the government-run boarding school as well. This traumatic introduction to boarding school was experienced by each student, and many such accounts exist. The interesting thing about Zitkala-Sa's account is that it was written by her, without a translator, and published in a well-regarded American magazine, *Atlantic Monthly*, in 1900, one year before Superintendent of Indian Schools Estelle Reel established her Uniform Course of Study for all government boarding school students.

The Cutting of My Long Hair

The first day in the land of apples was a bitter-cold one; for the snow still covered the ground, and the trees were bare. A large bell rang for breakfast, its loud metallic voice crashing through the belfry overhead and into our sensitive ears. The annoying clatter of shoes on bare floors gave us no peace. The constant clash of harsh noises, with an undercurrent of many voices murmuring an unknown tongue, made a bedlam within which I was securely tied. And though my spirit tore itself in struggling for its lost freedom, all was useless.

A paleface woman, with white hair, came up after us. We were placed in a line of girls who were marching into the dining room. These were Indian girls, in stiff shoes and closely clinging dresses. The small girls wore sleeved aprons and shingled hair. As I walked noiselessly in my soft moccasins, I felt like sinking to the floor, for my blanket had been stripped from my shoulders. I looked hard at the Indian girls, who seemed not to care that they were even more immodestly dressed than I, in their tightly fitting clothes. While we marched in, the boys entered at an opposite door. I watched for the three young braves who came in our party. I spied them in the rear ranks, looking as uncomfortable as I felt.

A small bell was tapped, and each of the pupils drew a chair from under the table. Supposing this act meant they were to be seated, I pulled out mine and at once slipped into it from one side. But when I turned my head, I saw that I was the only one seated, and all the rest at our table remained standing. Just as I began to rise, looking shyly around to see how chairs were to be used, a second bell was sounded. All were seated at last, and I had to crawl back into my chair again. I heard a man's voice at one end of the hall, and I looked around to see him. But all the others hung their heads over their plates. As I glanced at the long chain of tables, I caught the eyes of a paleface woman upon me. Immediately I dropped my eyes, wondering why I was so keenly watched by the strange woman. The man ceased his mutterings, and then a third bell was tapped. Everyone picked up his knife and fork and began eating. I began crying instead, for by this time I was afraid to venture anything more.

But this eating by formula was not the hardest trial in that first day. Late in the morning, my friend Judewin gave me a terrible warning. Judewin knew a few words of English; and she had overheard the paleface woman talk about cutting our long, heavy hair. Our mothers had taught us that only unskilled warriors who were captured had their hair shingled by the enemy. Among our people, short hair was worn by mourners, and shingled hair by cowards!

We discussed our fate some moments, and when Judewin said, "We have to submit, because they are strong," I rebelled.

"No, I will not submit! I will struggle first!" I answered.

I watched my chance, and when no one noticed I disappeared. I crept up the stairs as quietly as I could in my squeaking shoes,—my moccasins had been exchanged for shoes. Along the hall I passed, without knowing whither I was going. Turning aside to an open door, I found a large room with three white beds in it. The windows were covered with dark green curtains, which made the room very dim. Thankful that no one was there, I directed my steps toward the corner farthest from the door. On my hands and knees I crawled under the bed, and cuddled myself in the dark corner.

From my hiding place I peered out, shuddering with fear whenever I heard footsteps near by. Though in the hall loud voices were calling my name, and I knew that even Judewin was searching for me, I did not open my mouth to answer. Then the steps were quickened and the voices became excited. The sounds came nearer and nearer. Women and girls entered the room. I held my breath and watched them open closet doors and peep behind large trunks. Some one threw up the curtains, and the room was filled with sudden light. What caused them to stoop and look under the bed I do not know. I remember being dragged out, though I resisted by kicking and scratching wildly. In spite of myself, I was carried downstairs and tied fast in a chair.

I cried aloud, shaking my head all the while until I felt the cold blades of the scissors against my neck, and heard them gnaw off one of my thick braids. Then I lost my spirit. Since the day I was taken from my mother I had suffered extreme indignities. People had stared at me. I had been tossed about in the air like a wooden puppet. And now my long hair was shingled like a coward's! In my anguish I moaned for my mother, but no one came to comfort me. Not a soul reasoned quietly with me, as my own mother used to do; for now I was only one of many little animals driven by a herder.

Source: Zitkala-Sa. "The Cutting of My Long Hair." Chapter II of *School Days of an Indian Girl.* Boston and New York: Houghton, Mifflin and Company (1900): 185–87. Originally published in *Atlantic Monthly*, 85 (February 1900), 185–94.

───────────

EXTRACT FROM THE *ANNUAL REPORT OF THE COMMISSIONER OF INDIAN AFFAIRS*, OCTOBER 1, 1889

Thomas Morgan was appointed commissioner of Indian Affairs in 1889, and in this, his first annual report to Congress, he elaborates his beliefs about the direction of his office. Morgan was an ardent believer in assimilation as a strategy for dealing with the American Indians, as this excerpt from his Annual Report demonstrates.

First.—The anomalous position heretofore occupied by the Indians in this country can not much longer be maintained. The reservation system belongs to a "vanishing state of things" and must soon cease to exist.

Second.—The logic of events demands the absorption of the Indians into our national life, not as Indians, but as American citizens.

Third.—As soon as a wise conservatism will warrant it, the relations of the Indians to the Government must rest solely upon the full recognition of their individuality. Each Indian must be treated as a man, be allowed a man's rights and privileges, and be held to the performance of a man's obligations. Each Indian is entitled to his proper share of the inherited wealth of the tribe, and to the protection of the courts in his "life, liberty, and pursuit of happiness." He is not entitled to be supported in idleness.

Fourth.—The Indians must conform to "the white man's ways," peaceably if they will, forcibly if they must. They must adjust themselves to their environment, and conform their mode of living substantially to our civilization. This civilization may not be the best possible, but it is the best the Indians can get. They can not escape it, and must either conform to it or be crushed by it.

Fifth.—The paramount duty of the hour is to prepare the rising generation of Indians for the new order of things thus forced upon them.

A comprehensive system of education modeled after the American public-school system, but adapted to the special exigencies of the Indian youth, embracing all persons of school age, compulsory in its demands and uniformly administered, should be developed as rapidly as possible.

Sixth.—The tribal relations should be broken up, socialism destroyed, and the family and the autonomy of the individual substituted. The allotment of lands in severalty, the establishment of local courts and police, the development of a personal sense of independence, and the universal adoption of the English language are means to this end.

Seventh.—In the administration of Indian affairs there is need and opportunity for the exercise of the same qualities demanded in any other great administration—integrity, justice, patience, and good sense. Dishonesty, injustice, favoritism, and incompetency have no place here any more than elsewhere in the Government.

Eighth.—The chief thing to be considered in the administration of this office is the character of the men and women employed to carry out the designs of the Government. The best system may be perverted to bad ends by incompetent or dishonest persons employed to carry it into execution, while a very bad system may yield good results if wisely and honestly administered . . .

Source: Extract from the *Annual Report of the Commissioner of Indian Affairs* (1889). *House Executive Document* no. 1, 51st Cong., 1st sess., serial 2725, pp. 3–4. Available at http://www.alaskool.org/native_ed/historicdocs/use_of_english/prucha.htm#107.

THE PROBLEM OF INDIAN ADMINISTRATION: REPORT OF A SURVEY MADE AT THE REQUEST OF HONORABLE HUBERT WORK, SECRETARY OF THE INTERIOR, AND SUBMITTED TO HIM, FEBRUARY 21, 1928 (MERIAM REPORT)

Also known as the Meriam Report, named for Lewis Meriam, the principal investigator of the survey team created by the Institute of Government Research (later known as the Brookings Institution), this team examined conditions of the Native Americans across the country, visiting many schools and reservations during 1926–1928. Their resulting report addressed a general policy for Indian affairs, health, education, general economic conditions, family and community life, the migrated Indians, legal aspects of the "Indian Problem," and missionary activities among the Indians. The resulting 847-page report described the failure of the government to protect the Native Americans, their lands, and resources. This condemnation heralded a shift in American Indian policies and practices. The excerpts from that massive report that are reprinted here all come from the section of the report on education.

Meriam Report Excerpts: Chapter IX: Education

Fundamental Needs. The most fundamental need in Indian education is a change in point of view. Whatever may have been the official governmental attitude, education for the Indian in the past has proceeded largely on the theory that it is necessary to remove the Indian child as far as possible from his home environment; whereas the modern point of view in education and social work lays stress on upbringing in the natural setting of home and family life. The Indian educational enterprise is peculiarly in need of the kind of approach that recognizes this principle; that is, less concerned with a conventional school system and more with the understanding of human beings. It is impossible to visit Indian schools without feeling that on the whole they have been less touched than have better public schools by the newer knowledge of human behavior; that they reflect, for the most part, an attitude toward children characteristic of older city schools or of rural schools in backward sections; that they are distinctly below the accepted social and educational standards of school systems in most cities and the better rural communities.

Recognition of the Individual. It is true in all education, but especially in the education of people situated as are the American Indians, that methods must be adapted to individual abilities, interests, and needs. A standard course of study, routine classroom methods, traditional types of schools, even if they were adequately supplied—and they are not—would not solve the problem. The methods of the average public school in the United States cannot safely be taken over bodily and applied to Indian education. Indian tribes and individual Indians within the tribes vary so much that a standard content and method of education, no matter how carefully they might be prepared, would be worse than futile. Moreover, the standard course of study for Indian schools and the system of uniform examinations based upon it represent a procedure now no longer accepted by schools throughout the United States.

Better Personnel. The standards that are worthwhile in education are minimum standards, and the most successful American experience has made these apply, not primarily to courses of study and examination, but to qualifications of personnel. The surest way to achieve the change in point of view that is imperative in Indian education is to raise the qualifications of teachers and other employees. After all is said that can be said about the skill and devotion of some employees, the fact remains that the government of the United States regularly takes into the instructional staff of its Indian schools teachers whose credentials would not be accepted in good public school systems, and into the institutional side of these schools key employees—matrons and the like—who could not meet the standards set up by modern social agencies. A modernly equipped personnel would do more than any other one thing to bring necessary improvement."

Undesirable Effects of Routinization. The whole machinery of routinized boarding school and agency life works against the kind of initiative and independence, the development of which should be the chief concern of Indian education in and out of school. What all wish for is Indians who can take their place as independent citizens. The routinization characteristic of the boarding schools, with everything scheduled, no time left to be used at one's own initiative, every movement determined by a signal or an order, leads just the other way. It symbolizes a manner of treating Indians which will have to be abandoned if Indians, children and adults alike, are ever to become self-reliant members of the American community.

Can the Indian be "Educated"? It is necessary at this point to consider one question that is always raised in connection with an educational program for Indians: Is it really worth while to do anything for Indians, or are they an "inferior" race? Can the Indian be "educated"?

The question as usually asked implies, it should be noted, the restricted notion of education as mere formal schooling against which caution has already been pronounced; but whether schooling of the intellectual type is meant or education in the broader sense of desirable individual and social changes, the answer can be given unequivocally: *The Indian is essentially capable of education.*"

The Real Objectives of Education. Study of modern curriculum investigations will show that, while there are conflicting views as to whether the content of education shall be mainly quantities of subject matter transmitted or mainly experiences that will provide the child with means of development, yet there are certain principles hitherto disregarded that will have to be considered in any basic revision of the Indian school curriculum. One has already been referred to—the principle that emphasizes suggestion rather than prescription and allows teachers to adapt content to the needs and aptitudes of the children. Still another has to do with the objectives of education. The present course of study, notwithstanding its preliminary statements, in reality accepts the old notion of the "three R's" as fundamental in education. It is historically a mistake to say, as the Indian School Course of Study does, that from primitive times reading, writing, and arithmetic have formed the foundation of education. They have been the tools, undoubtedly, but long before they were used as tools there was education of the most important sort. The real goals of education are not "reading, writing, and arithmetic"—not even teaching Indians to speak English, though that is important—but sound health, both mental and physical, good citizenship in the sense of an understanding participation in community life, ability to earn one's own living honestly and efficiently in a socially worthwhile vocation, comfortable and desirable home and family life, and good character. These are the real aims of education; reading, writing, numbers, geography, history, and other "subjects" or skills are only useful to the extent that they contribute directly or indirectly to these fundamental objectives. With a course of study such as that provided for the Indian Service, with the limited time in which to carry it out as compared with ordinary schools, with teachers below the level of standard professional preparation, and with uniform old-type examinations at the end of the year as the only real goal at which to aim, the almost inevitable result is a highly mechanical content of education handled in a mechanical way."

School Organization in the Indian Service. In an effort to furnish Indian boys and girls with a type of education that would be practical and cost little, the government years ago adopted for the boarding schools a half-time plan whereby pupils spend half the school day in "academic" subjects and the remaining half day in work about the institution. Some of the best educational programs for any people have been built upon some such provision of work opportunities. As administered at present in the Indian Service, however, this otherwise useful method has lost much of its effectiveness and has probably become a menace to both health and education.

A Full-Day Educational Program Needed. Pupils of the first six grades in Indian schools should be in school all day. Indeed, if the right kind of educational program is provided, that is, not limited to "academic" subjects, it may safely be said that, except for conspicuously over-age children, the Indian school should as a minimum approximate the opportunities for other children by regarding the years through 14, at least, as primarily for education, and not for "work" in the adult sense.

Industrial and Agricultural Education. The first need in industrial and agricultural education in Indian schools is a survey to find out what Indian young people are doing when they get out of school and what the occupational opportunities for them are. This involves a study of new industries as well as the adaptation of old ones, and the establishment of a training program based upon the findings. The Course of Study and the literature generally of the Indian Office insist that Indian education is essentially "vocational," and "vocational guidance" is regarded as "of such great moment that each school is directed to establish a vocational guidance committee which shall consist of the superintendent as chairman and not less than three other members appointed by him." Actually, however, very little of the work provided in Indian boarding schools is directly vocational in the sense that it is aimed at a specific vocation which the youngster is to pursue or based upon a study of known industrial opportunities, and vocational direction in the form of proper guidance, placement, and follow-up hardly exists at all."

The Outing System. The nearest approach in the Indian Service to the cooperative part-time plan is the so-called "outing system," which, originally established at the old Carlisle School, Carlisle, Pennsylvania, is still praised by graduates of that institution wherever one finds them. Its possibilities for specific vocational training have hardly ever been given a fair trial. Whatever it may have been in the past, at present the outing system is mainly a plan for hiring out boys for odd jobs and girls for domestic service, seldom a plan for providing real vocational training.

Health Conditions at the Schools. The deplorable health conditions at most of the schools have been sufficiently described in the chapter on Health of this report. Old buildings, often kept in use long after they should have been pulled down, and admittedly bad fire-risks in many instances; crowded dormitories; conditions of sanitation that are usually perhaps as good as they can be under the circumstances, but certainly below accepted standards; boilers and machinery out-of-date and in some instances unsafe, to the point of having long since been condemned, but never replaced; many medical officers who are of low standards of training and relatively unacquainted with the methods of modern medicine, to say nothing of health education for children; lack of milk sufficient to give children anything like the official "standard" of a quart per child per day, almost none of the fresh fruits and vegetables that are recommended as necessary in the menus taught to the children in the classroom; the serious malnutrition, due to the lack of food and use of wrong foods; schoolrooms seldom showing knowledge of modern principles of lighting and ventilating;

lack of recreational opportunities, except athletics for a relatively small number in the larger schools; an abnormally long day, which cuts to a dangerous point the normal allowance for sleep and rest, especially for small children; and the generally routinized nature of the institutional life with its formalism in classrooms, its marching and dress parades, its annihilation of initiative, its lack of beauty, its almost complete negation of normal family life, all of which have disastrous effects upon mental health and the development of wholesome personality: These are some of the conditions that make even the best classroom teaching of health ineffective. Building up of health habits is at the basis of any genuine health educational program, and right health habits cannot develop where all the surroundings pull the other way. Some conspicuous exceptions, of course, must be noted to this general indictment: a few schools where there is milk in abundance; possibly one or two where most of the buildings are in good condition; and an occasional one where the children show the effect of natural human handling and are not as restrained and shy as they usually are. In almost no case, however, could a reasonably clean bill of health be given to any one school. It happens that a school with one of the finest-looking plants in the service is at the same time one of the least satisfactory in the physical condition of its children and in routinization; and in one school, that is conspicuous for its delightful handling of orphan children, the school authorities recently stopped testing their water supply because it regularly showed contamination.

Source: Lewis Meriam, Ray A. Brown, Henry Roe Cloud, et. al. *The Problem of Indian Administration: Report of a Survey made at the request of Honorable Hubert Work, Secretary of the Interior, and submitted to him, February 21, 1928.* Baltimore: Johns Hopkins Press, 1928. Available at: http://www.alaskool.org/native_ed/research_reports/IndianAdmin/Indian_Admin_Problms.html.

Glossary

Aboriginal: The first or original people to inhabit an area.

Allotment: Apportionment, or dividing up equally. Under the Dawes Act, the reservation lands held communally by Native American tribes were apportioned among the tribal members, with leftover lands reverting to the government. This resulted in further losses of land for the Native Americans.

Appropriation: Money set aside by formal action of the U.S. Congress for a particular use (i.e., to fund budgets for government boarding schools).

Assimilation: To be taken in to become a part of the whole; for the Native Americans it meant to become absorbed into, and indistinguishable from, the mainstream Anglo-American culture.

Charter: A granting of rights and privileges from the sovereign power or ruling country. When the United States existed as an English colony, establishing institutions was accomplished through a charter being granted by the British monarchy.

Conversion: The official adoption of a particular religion, in this case, some form of Christianity.

Decimate: To reduce the population drastically; or to cause great destruction and harm.

Demerit: A mark placed against a student's record for some offense that results in punishment or loss of privileges in order to erase the mark.

Denominational: Referring to a particular religious group that consists of a group of people with particular shared beliefs. In this case, boarding schools were established and run by the various Christian denominations, including Quaker, Mennonite, Catholic, etc.

Divestiture: The forced transfer of title or sale of interests because of a government order. For example, treaties were used to divest the Native Americans of their traditional lands.

Exacerbate: To make more violent, bitter, or severe; to make a bad situation worse.

Exhort: To influence someone by strongly urging them toward a particular course of action.

Immersion: To become completely surrounded by and absorbed in something; to learn a language by hearing only that language. The boarding school students were *immersed* in the Anglo-American language and culture in order to learn it rapidly.

Indigenous: Living or occurring naturally in a particular environment; the Native Americans are indigenous to North America, and the Anglo-Americans are not indigenous.

Outing Program: A program conceived by Colonel Pratt at the Carlisle boarding school whereby students would spend their summers living with and working for an Anglo-American family for a stipend. Pratt envisioned the results of such a program would be that the student's immersion in Anglo-American culture would advance their assimilation, and they would earn money at the same time. The family would gain a respect and appreciation for the capabilities of the Native American student.

Pan-Indianism: A philosophy and sociopolitical movement promoting unity and solidarity among different American Indians regardless of tribal affiliations; a banding together of different tribes for the betterment of all Native American people.

Populace: The population, or the masses of common people.

Progressives (Friendlies):   Referring to those Native American parents who advocated and promoted Anglo-American education for their children as beneficial.

Relinquish: To give up possession and control of; the Native Americans *relinquished* the title to their lands in treaties with the United States after military defeat.

Removal: To change the location of; to eliminate. Also, U.S. government policy of exchanging traditional Native American tribal lands usually located in the eastern United States for other lands farther west through treaty and intimidation; forcing relocation of tribes off lands desired by Anglo-Americans.

Reservation: Set aside or reserved for special use; the U.S. government set aside lands specifically and only for the use of Native American tribes in treaties with the tribes, and these lands are called reservations.

Self-determination: Free choice; determination by a group of people of their own status, governance, and institutions. For Native Americans, the ability to govern themselves and to establish and direct their own educational institutions represented one aspect of self-determination.

Subsidize: To pay for with government funds. Historically, American Indians were not able to attend public schools because they were not required to pay taxes. When the Johnson-O'Malley Act subsidized public education for Native Americans, they were able to attend any public school, which allowed them to become educated outside the boarding school system.

Termination: A government policy vis-à-vis the American Indians that ended the special relationship between the tribes and the U.S. government, making them ordinary U.S. citizens. The practical results included the end of the government's recognition of tribal sovereignty, the end of Indian reservations, and the end of exemption from state laws and federal tax laws. This policy was detrimental to Native American self-determination.

Traditionals (Hostiles):   Referring to those Native American parents who resisted Anglo-American education for their children, often to the point of hiding their children from officials and serving jail terms for not complying with compulsory education.

Annotated Bibliography

Audiovisual

Contrary Warrior: The Life and Times of Adam Fortunate Eagle. **Lillimar Pictures presents a film by John Ferry, 2010.**

This documentary features the elder Fortunate Eagle speaking about his life, including his childhood at the Pipestone boarding school, his participation in the takeover of Alcatraz Island in the 1960s, and his life as an activist and artist.

Our Spirits Don't Speak English: Indian Boarding School. **Rich-Heape Films, 2008.**

A documentary by a native-owned production company tells the story of the American movement to place Native American children in boarding schools and the resulting assault on their language and culture in boarding schools. Includes interviews with people who have lived in and survived boarding schools.

Books

Adams, David Wallace. *Education for Extinction: American Indians and the Boarding School Experience, 1875–1928.* **Lawrence: University Press of Kansas, 1995.**

A scholarly history of the American Indian boarding school era, emphasizing the philosophy of acculturation behind the educational experience, and the responses of the Native American students.

Archuleta, Margaret L., Brenda J. Child, and K. Tsianina Lomawaima, eds. *Away from Home: American Indian Boarding School Experiences, 1879–2000.* **Phoenix: Heard Museum, 2000.**

The Heard Museum held an exhibition about Native American boarding schools called "Remembering Our Indian School Days: The Boarding School Experience," and commissioned this book to accompany the exhibit, written by experts in the field, and containing many photographs.

Ball, Eve. *Indeh: An Apache Odyssey.* Norman: University of Oklahoma Press, 1980.

An oral history of the Chiricahua Apaches as told to Eve Ball by the survivors who were imprisoned in Florida and then sent to Fort Sill. Among them were individuals who were sent to Carlisle Indian Boarding School.

Berkhofer, Robert F. *Salvation and the Savage: An Analysis of Protestant Missions and American Indian Response, 1787–1862.* New York: Atheneum, 1972.

A history of Protestant missions among the American Indians, including their educational boarding schools, just prior to the establishment of government boarding schools for Native Americans.

Bonnell, Sonciray. *Chemawa Indian Boarding School: The First One Hundred Years, 1880–1980.* N.P.: Dissertation.com, 1997.

A history of Chemawa Indian boarding school told through interviews of its graduates; this is a scholarly dissertation.

Bowden, Henry Warner. *American Indians and Christian Missions: Studies in Cultural Conflict.* Chicago: University of Chicago Press, 1981.

A scholarly history of Christian missions among the American Indians throughout history; starting with Spanish, French, and English missions prior to the American Revolution, and continuing with the post-Revolution American missions by century.

Butler, Jon. *Religion in Colonial America.* New York: Oxford University Press, 2000.

A scholarly history of early religious pluralism in the American colonies, and what this meant for the Native Americans already in residence.

Child, Brenda J. *Boarding School Seasons: American Indian Families, 1900–1940.* Lincoln: University of Nebraska Press, 1998.

Educator and historian Child uses previously unpublished letters from Flandrau and Haskell boarding school students, parents, and administrators to illustrate the boarding school experience.

Coleman, Michael C. *American Indian Children at School, 1850–1930.* **Jackson: University Press of Mississippi, 1993.**

This analysis of boarding school life is based on autobiographical accounts written by Native Americans who attended boarding school.

Cooper, Michael L. *Indian School: Teaching the White Man's Way.* **New York: Clarion Books, 1999.**

A brief history of Indian boarding schools written for grades 4–8, which contains many photographs.

Fortunate Eagle, Adam. *Pipestone: My Life in an Indian Boarding School.* **Norman: University of Oklahoma Press, 2010.**

Fortunate Eagle's memoir of his boarding school life at Pipestone from 1935 to 1945.

Golden, Gertrude. *Red Moon Called Me: Memoirs of a Schoolteacher in the Government Indian Service.* **San Antonio: Naylor, 1954.**

Gertrude Golden was one of the single white female schoolteachers sent by the Indian Service to teach Native American children in schools in remote locations. She taught for 17 years in Indian schools in five different western states. Her book contains the writings of her students in the chapter entitled "Let the Children Speak."

Horne, Esther Burnett, and Sally McBeth. *Essie's Story: The Life and Legacy of a Shoshone Teacher.* **Lincoln: University of Nebraska Press, 1998.**

This memoir, written by Essie Horne, covers her school years at the Haskell Institute as a student and her subsequent career as a boarding school educator at Wahpeton. She was inspired by her Native American teachers to become an educator.

Littlefield, Holly. *Children of the Indian Boarding Schools.* **Minneapolis: Carolrhoda Books, 2001.**

In a book written for children in grades 2–4, Littlefield uses historical photographs paired with simple text to tell the story of American Indian boarding schools.

Lomawaima, K. Tsianina. *They Called It Prairie Light: The Story of Chilocco Indian School*. Lincoln: University of Nebraska Press, 1994.

Historian and educator Lomawaima tells the history of Chilocco Indian School through interviews of former students, including her father.

Lomawaima, Tsianina. "The Unnatural History of American Indian Education." In *Next Steps: Research and Practice to Advance Indian Education*, edited by Karen Gayton Swisher and John W. Tippeconnic. Washington, DC: ERIC, 1999.

In this article, Lomawaima elucidates the four basic tenets of the early colonists' educational philosophy vis a vis the Native Americans.

Lomawaima, K. Tsianina, and Teresa L. McCarty. *"To Remain an Indian": Lessons in Democracy from a Century of Native American Education*. New York: Teachers College Press, 2006.

This book traces the history of Native American education from the original native model through government boarding schools to the present day. The dizzying shifts in U.S. educational policy vis-à-vis the Native Americans are explained by the authors' safety zone theory.

McCarty, Teresa L. *A Place to Be Navajo: Rough Rock and the Struggle for Self-Determination in Indigenous Schooling*. Mahwah, NJ: Lawrence Erlbaum, 2002.

Educator Teresa McCarty writes the biography of the first Native American community-controlled school program on the Navajo Nation, beginning in 1966, and traces its development to the present time in this scholarly, compassionate work.

McDade, Jeffrey R. *The Birth of the American Indian Manual Labor Boarding School: Social Control Through Culture Destruction, 1820–1850*. Lewiston, NY: Edwin Mellen, 2008.

Dr. McDade examines Native American boarding schools in the context of other institutions of social control such as prisons, asylums, and orphanages established by the dominant society.

Parker, Dorothy R. *Phoenix Indian School: The Second Half-Century.* **Tucson: University of Arizona Press, 1996.**

Parker's history of Phoenix Indian School covers the years 1930–1990 and takes up where Trennert's history leaves off.

Peyer, Bernd C., ed. *American Indian Nonfiction: An Anthology of Writings, 1760s–1930s.* **Norman: University of Oklahoma Press, 2007.**

A collection of primary resources; nonfiction prose written by Native Americans in English from 1760 forward, including the writings of Samson Occom.

Phillips, Joyce B., and Paul Gary Phillips, eds. *The Brainerd Journal: A Mission to the Cherokees, 1817–1823.* **Lincoln: University of Nebraska Press, 1998.**

A valuable primary resource, the missionaries in the interdenominational mission to the Cherokees in what is present-day Tennessee, recorded thoughts, actions, and routines of their daily lives in a journal kept by the mission.

Pratt, Richard Henry. *Battlefield and Classroom: Four Decades with the American Indian, 1867–1904.* **New Haven, CT: Yale University Press, 1964.**

Colonel Pratt's memoir contains his views on Native American education and his version of the history of Carlisle Indian boarding school, which he founded, and which was the first off-reservation, government-run boarding school for Native American children. His school remained the model for all those that followed.

Reyes, Lawney L. *White Grizzly Bear's Legacy: Learning to Be Indian.* **Seattle: University of Washington Press, 2002.**

Lawney Reyes's memoir includes chapters about his time spent as a student at Chemawa Indian Boarding School in Oregon.

Reyhner, Jon, and Jeanne Eder. *American Indian Education: A History.* **Norman: University of Oklahoma Press, 2004.**

A comprehensive history of Native American education in the United States from colonial times to the present.

Sekaquaptewa, Helen. *Me and Mine: The Life Story of Helen Sekaquaptewa as told to Louise Udall.* **Tucson: University of Arizona Press, 1969.**

This memoir of an Arizona Hopi woman includes her years spent as a student at the Phoenix Indian School.

Standing Bear, Luther. *Land of the Spotted Eagle.* **Boston: Houghton Mifflin, 1933.**

This book by Standing Bear describes the Lakota lifestyle, and contains an account of Standing Bear's youth as well as his views on education and the place of Native Americans in the United States.

Standing Bear, Luther. *My Indian Boyhood.* **New ed. Lincoln: University of Nebraska Press, 1931.**

One of the original Carlisle students wrote and published his memoirs in three volumes. This volume deals with his home life and education, as well as his experiences at Carlisle boarding school.

Standing Bear, Luther. *My People, the Sioux.* **New ed. Lincoln: University of Nebraska Press, 1975.**

Standing Bear's book about his tribe is primarily autobiographical in nature; originally published in 1928. This book contains his thoughts and philosophies about education, as well as a native point of view on the historical times he lived through.

Stein, Wayne J. *Tribally Controlled Colleges: Making Good Medicine.* **New York: Peter Lang, 1992.**

Describes the emergence of tribally controlled colleges on the American educational scene, including case studies of individual colleges.

Szasz, Margaret Connell. *Education and the American Indian: The Road to Self-Determination Since 1928.* **3rd ed., rev. and enl. Albuquerque: University of New Mexico Press, 1999.**

A history of federal policies regarding American Indian education, following their implications and results.

Szasz, Margaret Connell. *Indian Education In the American Colonies, 1607–1783.* **Albuquerque: University of New Mexico Press, 1988.**

A comprehensive, scholarly exploration of the American colonists' educational efforts vis-à-vis the Native Americans in early colonial America.

Trafzer, Clifford E., Jean A. Keller, and Lorene Sisquoc, eds. *Boarding School Blues: Revisiting American Indian Educational Experiences.* **Lincoln: University of Nebraska Press, 2006.**

A collection of scholarly essays about various aspects of the Native American boarding school experience, revealing both the light and the dark sides of boarding schools.

Trennert, Robert A. *Phoenix Indian School: Forced Assimilation in Arizona, 1891–1935.* **Norman: University of Oklahoma Press, 1988.**

Scholarly history of the Phoenix Indian School through 1935.

Vuckovic, Myriam. *Voices from Haskell: Indian Students Between Two Worlds, 1884–1928.* **Lawrence: University Press of Kansas, 2008.**

A history of the Haskell boarding school in Kansas, told through the words and letters of the students.

Welch, Deborah. "Gertrude Simmons Bonnin (Zitkala-Shceka): Dakota." In *The New Warriors: Native American Leaders Since 1900,* **edited by David Edmunds. Lincoln: University of Nebraska Press, 2001): 35–54.**

Biography of Zitkaka-Sa.

Zitkala-Sa. *American Indian Stories.* **Reprint. Lincoln: University of Nebraska Press, 1985.**

Contains stories, including autobiographical stories, by the author who attended a mission boarding school and went on to teach at Carlisle and to become an early activist for Native American rights. Originally published in 1921.

Articles

Andrew, John. "Educating the Heathen: The Foreign Mission School Controversy and American Ideals." *Journal of American Studies* **12, no. 3 (December 1978): 331–42.**

An account of the controversy at the Foreign Mission School when Harriet Gold married Elias Boudinot, a Cherokee student, and the impact on the school.

Berkhofer, Robert. "Model Zions for the American Indian." *American Quarterly* **15, no. 2, part 1 (summer 1963): 176–90.**

An examination of the manual labor boarding schools established for the Native American children by the missionaries during the 1800s; the precursors to the government-run boarding schools.

Bloom, John. "Show What an Indian Can Do: Sports, Memory, and Ethnic Identity at Federal Indian Boarding Schools." *Journal of American Indian Education* **35, no. 3 (spring 1996) http://jaie.asu.edu/v35/ V35S3sh.htm.**

Bloom examines the sports programs of the boarding schools, which produced some extraordinary athletes, and observes the importance of ethnic pride in the team competitions. Many student memoirs express positive memories of their schools' sports programs.

Bohl, Sarah R. "Wyoming's Estelle Reel: The First Woman Elected to a Statewide Office in America." *Annals of Wyoming: The Wyoming History Journal* **75 (winter 2003). http://uwacadweb.uwyo.edu/robertshis tory/estelle_reel.htm.**

A biographical article about Estelle Reel, one of the superintendents of Indian schools during the government boarding school era.

Child, Brenda. "Runaway Boys, Resistant Girls: Rebellion at Flandreau and Haskell, 1900–1940." *Journal of American Indian Education* **35, no. 3 (spring 1996). http://jaie.asu.edu/v35/V35S3run.htm.**

Historian Brenda Child addresses the results of frustrations with the Indian boarding schools—runaways and other types of rebellion on the part of the students. Her use of student letters in their own words is evocative and descriptive of the depths of their feelings.

Davis, Julie. "American Indian Boarding School Experiences: Recent Studies from Native Perspectives." *OAH Magazine of History* **15, no. 2 (winter 2001): 20–22.**

A brief review of the contemporary research on American Indian boarding schools.

Lomawaima, K. Tsianina. "Domesticity in the Federal Indian Schools: The Power of Authority over Mind and Body." *American Ethnologist* 20, no. 2 (May 1993): 227–40.

Lomawaima contends that the domestic training given Native American women in boarding schools was not for the purpose of assimilation into the dominant society but to train them to become obedient manual laborers.

Lomawaima, K. Tsianina. "Estelle Reel, Superintendent of Indian Schools, 1898–1910: Politics, Curriculum, and Land." *Journal of American Indian Education* 35, no. 3 (May 1996). http://jaie.asu.edu/v35/V35S3es.htm.

This article examines the career of the first female superintendent of Indian Schools and how her prejudices, attitudes, and political aspirations influenced the curriculum and administration of the Indian boarding schools she supervised.

Lomawaima, K. Tsianina. "Oral Histories from Chilocco Indian Agricultural School, 1920–1940." *American Indian Quarterly* 11, no. 3 (summer 1987): 241–54.

Lomawaima uses oral histories from former students as the lens to view the Chilocco boarding school, a school with a "culture created and sustained by its student population."

Morton, Louis. "How the Indians Came to Carlisle." *Pennsylvania History* 29, no. 1 (January 1962): 53–73.

An in-depth, historical account of the opening of Carlisle Indian School in Pennsylvania by Colonel Pratt.

Trennert, Robert A. "'And the Sword Will Give Way to the Spelling-Book': Establishing the Phoenix Indian School." *Journal of Arizona History* 23 (spring 1982): 35–58.

A detailed account of how the Phoenix Indian School began.

Trennert, Robert A. "Corporal Punishment and the Politics of Indian Reform." *History of Education Quarterly* 29, no. 4 (winter 1989), 595–617.

The author examines the alleged instances of corporal punishment at the Phoenix Indian School and how they became fodder for Collier's reform movement.

Trennert, Robert A. "From Carlisle to Phoenix: The Rise and Fall of the Indian Outing System, 1878–1930." *Pacific Historical Review* 52 (1983): 267–91.

The outing system, an apprenticeship program established originally at Carlisle Indian School by Colonel Pratt, is examined as it changed through time, and the differences between the Carlisle and Phoenix models of this program are explored.

Trennert, Robert A. "Peaceably If They Will, Forcibly If They Must: The Phoenix Indian School, 1890–1901." *Journal of Arizona History* 20 (autumn 1979): 297–322.

The first 10 years of the Phoenix Indian School are examined in this article.

Warren, Kim. "'All Indian Trails Lead to Lawrence, October 27 to 30, 1926': American Identity and the Dedication of Haskell Institute's Football Stadium." *Kansas History: A Journal of the Central Plains* 30 (spring 2007): 2–19.

The author describes the significance of an enormous homecoming/fundraising celebration for Haskell alumni, which resulted in the opening of a new football stadium.

Government Documents

U.S. Bureau of Education. *The Indian School: Carlisle Barracks.* Washington, DC: Government Printing Office, 1880.

A government report issued on the progress of Carlisle Indian School four months after its inception in 1879.

U.S. Superintendent of Indian Schools. *Report of the Superintendent of Indian Schools to the Commissioner of Indian Affairs for the year ended . . .* Washington, DC: Government Printing Office.

This annual report to the Commissioner contains the primary documentation of the superintendent, who was charged with overseeing and inspecting all of the government-controlled boarding schools. For the year 1901, this report contains Estelle Reel's Uniform Course of Study, as well as her reports on all the boarding schools she visited and inspected during the year.

U.S. White House Conference on Indian Education (January 1992). ***The Final Report of the White House Conference on Indian Education: Executive Summary, May 22, 1992.*** **Washington, DC: White House Conference on Indian Education, 1992.**

This executive summary contains a list of final resolutions adopted by the White House Conference and a summary of the outcomes of the conference.

Websites

American Indian Higher Education Consortium. **http://www.aihec.org/.**

The official website of the American Indian Higher Education Consortium.

Boarding School Healing Project. **http://www.boardingschoolhealing project.org/index.html.**

This website is for those who seek healing from the trauma of boarding school, and who are taking action to seek reparations from the U.S. government for the damages inflicted by the boarding schools.

Chemawa Indian School. **http://www.chemawa.bie.edu/.**

This is the official website of the school, the oldest boarding school for Native Americans that is still in existence today.

"Chemawa Indian School." *Salem Online History.* **http://www.salem history.net/education/chemawa.htm.**

History of the Chemawa Indian School

Chilocco National Alumni Association. *Chilocco Indian School Alumni.* **http://www.chilocco.org/.**

Since the Chilocco campus is closed, this website provides updates about plans for the former school site, raises funds, and announces reunions, which continue on an annual basis.

"Cultural Genocide and Education: The Story of the Carlisle Indian Industrial School." *Adventures in Free Schooling.* November 14, 2008. http://freeschools.wordpress.com/2008/11/14/cultural-genocide-and-education-the-story-of-the-carlisle-indian-industrial-school/.

An unattributed essay on the Carlisle Indian School.

Diné College: The Higher Education Institution of the Navajo Since 1968. http://www.dinecollege/edu.

History and other information about Diné College, the first tribally controlled community college in the United States.

Foreign Mission School. http://www.cornwallhistoricalsociety.org/foreign_mission_school.htm.

Gives the history of the Foreign Mission School in Connecticut.

Haskell Indian Nations University. http://www.haskell.edu.

"About Haskell" contains historical information about the school.

Indian Country Diaries: History: Indian Boarding Schools. http://www.pbs.org/indiancountry/history/boarding.html.

This interactive website provides information about Indian boarding schools as a background to the documentary about contemporary Native Americans *Indian Country Diaries.*

Kalambakal, Vickey. "Bibliography of Indian Boarding Schools: Approximately 1875 to 1940." *ASU Libraries: Labriola Center.* http://www.asu.edu/lib/archives/boardingschools.htm.

A finding guide to resources about Native American boarding schools at the Arizona State University Libraries and elsewhere. This annotated bibliography contains many useful sources.

Lakhota.com. "History of Indian Boarding Schools." *Kumeyaay Information Village Website.* http://www.kumeyaay.info/history/History_Indian_Boarding_Schools.pdf.

A pictorial look at the various Indian boarding schools from a California indigenous website.

Landis, Barbara. *Carlisle Indian Industrial School (1879–1918).* http://home.epix.net/~landis/index.html.

This web page by the Carlisle Indian School biographer is full of excellent, well-researched and well-presented information.

"Phoenix Indian School." http://en.wikipedia.org/wiki/Phoenix_Indian_School.

Contains facts and history about the now-defunct Phoenix Indian School.

Salgado, Ernie C. "Indian Boarding Schools." *California Indian Education.* http://www.californiaindianeducation.org/indian_boarding_schools/.

A blog outlining research resources on the topic of Indian boarding schools.

U.S. National Register of Historic Places. *Chilocco Indian Agricultural School.* http://www.cr.nps.gov/nr/feature/indian/2006/chilocco.htm.

Although it is no longer open, its buildings are listed in the National Park Service's Register of Historic Places. This web page contains history and photographs.

American Indian Boarding Schools in the United States, 1900/1901

The annual report of the commissioner of Indian Affairs for the year 1901 gave statistics about the education of Native American children. At that time, there were 25 off-reservation boarding schools administered by the government. The total enrollment for those boarding schools for this year was 7,928, although the capacity of the boarding schools is recorded as 7,315. The off-reservation boarding schools were located in the following places:

Albuquerque, New Mexico
Carlisle, Pennsylvania
Carson, Nevada
Chamberlain, South Dakota
Chemawa, Oregon
Chilocco, Oklahoma
Flandreau, South Dakota
Fort Bidwell, California
Fort Lewis, Colorado
Fort Mohave, Arizona
Fort Shaw, Montana
Genoa, Nebraska
Grand Junction, Colorado
Greenville, California
Lawrence, Kansas (Haskell Institute)
Morris, Minnesota
Mount Pleasant, Michigan
Perris, California
Phoenix, Arizona
Pierre, South Dakota

Pipestone, Minnesota
Rapid City, South Dakota
Santa Fe, New Mexico
Tomah, Wisconsin
Wittenberg, Wisconsin

In addition to the 25 off-reservation government boarding schools that year, there were 88 government-run boarding schools located on the various reservations, with a total enrollment of 10,782 pupils; these schools were much smaller than the off-reservation boarding schools listed above. A third class of schools was referred to as government day schools, which were government-supported schools located on the reservations and attended by day only, with the pupils returning home after school. In 1901, there were 128 government day schools with a total enrollment of 4,622 pupils. These schools were smaller than either the off-reservation boarding schools or the reservation boarding schools.

Tribally Controlled Colleges: AIHEC Members in 2011

The American Indian Higher Education Consortium is an organization whose membership is colleges that are tribally controlled. Originally established in 1972 as a network of schools seeking to present a united message about Native American education to the U.S. government in an effort to influence government educational policy, the organization continues with its mission to support Native American self-determination through the establishment and support of tribally controlled institutions of higher education.

Regular Members

Aaniiih Nakoda College (formerly Fort Belknap College)
Bay Mills Community College
Blackfeet Community College
Cankdeska Cikana Community College
Chief Dull Knife College
College of Menominee Nation
Diné College
Fond du Lac Tribal and Community College
Fort Berthold Community College
Fort Peck Community College
Haskell Indian Nations University
Ilisagvik College
Institute of American Indian Arts
Keweenaw Bay Ojibwa Community College
Lac Courte Oreilles Ojibwa Community College
Leech Lake Tribal College
Little Big Horn College
Little Priest Tribal College

Navajo Technical College
Nebraska Indian Community College
Northwest Indian College
Oglala Lakota College
Saginaw Chippewa Tribal College
Salish Kootenai College
Sinte Gleska University
Sisseton Wahpeton College
Sitting Bull College
Southwestern Indian Polytechnic Institute
Stone Child College
Tohono O'odham Community College
Turtle Mountain Community College
United Tribes Technical College
White Earth Tribal and Community College

Associate Members

College of the Muscogee Nation
Comanche Nation College
Wind River Tribal College

Index

Aboriginal, 183
Adams, David Wallace, 62
Alaska Natives, 109, 116; at Chemawa, 78, 85
Alcatraz takeover (1969), 135
Alford, Thomas, 122
Algonquian language, 5
Algonquian tribes, 2
All Indian Pueblo Council, 110
Allotment, 183; Dawes Act, 47, 183; Indian Reorganization Act, 106
American Board of Commissioners for Foreign Missions (ABCFM), 15, 23
American Indian and Alaska Native Education Executive Order (1998), 109, 116
American Indian College Fund, 115
American Indian Higher Education Consortium, 115, 127
American Indians Veterans Memorial, 100
Apache prisoners: at Carlisle, 35–36
Appropriation, 183
Arizona: reservation land, 97
Arizona Interscholastic Association, 91
Arizona National Guard, 88
Arrival experiences, 32, 34, 35–36, 37, 75–76, 169–70; Zitkala-Sa, 173–76

Assimilation, 73, 74, 94, 183; at boarding schools, 48, 103, 105, 119; at Carlisle Indian School, 44; Kennedy Report (1969), 106; outing programs, 64–65, 184; Thomas Morgan on, 176–77
Attendance issues, 14

Beatty, William, 74
Begay, Yazzie, 114
Belt line, 68
Bible, Algonquian translation of, 5
Blair, Rev. James, 2–4
Boarding School Healing Project, 130
Boarding schools: attendance issues, 14; legacy of, 119–31. *See also* Mission schools; Native American boarding schools; Off-reservation boarding schools; Reservation schools
Board of Indian Commissioners, 24; returned student survey (1916), 124–25
Bonnin, Gertrude Simmons. *See* Zitkala-Sa
Bonnin, Raymond, 145
Boudinot, Elias (Galagina), 21, 22, 133–35
Boudinot, Harriet Gold, 21, 22, 133–34

Choctaw Indians: at Chilocco Indian Agricultural School, 71; at Foreign Mission School, 20; tribal-run schools, 24

Cholera, 23

Citizenship: Native Americans, 61–62

Civil service hiring system, 44

Clinton, President Bill, 109, 116

Cockenoe, 5

Coleman, Michael, 121–22

College of William and Mary (Virginia), 2

Colleges: Native American enrollment, 109–10

Collier, John, 74, 88, 94, 95, 146

Colonial period, 1–11; charters, 183

Colorado River Indians: Phoenix Indian Industrial School, 90

Colville Confederation Tribes, 141

Colville Indian Reservation (Washington), 141, 142

Comanche Indians: Carlisle students, 30

Comprehensive Federal Indian Education Policy Statement, 116

Congregational church, 15; Brainerd Mission School, 16

Conversion, 183

Cornwall, Connecticut: Foreign Mission School, 20–21

Corporal punishment, 68; at Phoenix Indian School, 93–94, 95

Council of Confederated Chilocco Tribes, 71

Crane, Leo, 122–24

Creek Indians: at Chilocco Indian Agricultural School, 71; tribal-run schools, 24

Cultural genocide: at boarding schools, 125, 129; Pratt's practices, 139

Cultural mediators: boarding school students as, 129–30

Daklugie, 35–36

Dartmouth College, 1, 8, 136–37

Dawes Allotment Act (1887), 47, 183

Day schools, 14

Deloria, Ella, 54, 55

Demerits, 84, 183

Dental disease, 58

Department of the Interior: Indian affairs investigation, 94

Desertion: from boarding schools, 69

Diné College. *See* Navajo Community College

Discipline: at Chilocco Indian School, 70–71; at Phoenix Indian School, 93–94, 95; at Pipestone, 84

Divestiture, 184

Domestic arts: at Pipestone, 79. *See also* Housekeeping; Laundry

Donner Foundation, 113

Duran, Jacob, 95

Earlham College (Indiana), 145

East Farm Sanatorium (Arizona), 96

Education: and self-determination, 185

Education policies, federal, 115–16; 20th century, 104, 105–9

Eliot, Rev. John, 5

Erickson, Donald, 111

First Nations boarding schools, 130

Flandrau boarding school (South Dakota), 68

Flogging, 95

Wenatchee Junior College, 142
Western frontier: Indian missions, 23
Wheeler, Ruth, 143
Wheeler-Howard Act. *See* Indian
  Reorganization Act (1934)
Wheelock, Eleazar, 6–9, 136–37
Whitaker, Rev. Nathaniel, 136
White House Conference on Indian
  Education (1992), 108–9, 158–66
White's Manual Labor Institute (Indi-
  ana), 36, 144
Worcester, Samuel, 21
Worcester v. Georgia (1832), 134
World War I: and Native Ameri-
  can education, 79–80; Native

American servicemen and citizen-
  ship, 61–62
Wowaus (James Printer), 5, 6
Wyoming: and Estelle Reed, 139–40

Yamasee Prince. *See* Prince George
Yankton Reservation (South
  Dakota), 144
Yazzie, Allen D., 110

Zah, Peterson, 91, 122
Zitkala-Sa (Gertrude Simmons Bonnin), 36–37, 43, 122, 123, 126, 130,
  144–46, 167; arrival experience,
  173–76

About the Author

MARY A. STOUT is a recently retired academic librarian and freelance writer with a M.A. in American Indian studies. Her previous works include *Geronimo: A Biography* (2009), and several children's books about various Native American tribes, including *Hopi* (2005) and *Shoshone* (2005).